Pit Stops *for* Peak Performance

Pit Stops
for Peak
Performance

The Pit Stop Formula for Managers
to Achieve Effortless High Performance

Kanti Gopal Kovvali

JAICO PUBLISHING HOUSE

Ahmedabad Bangalore Bhopal Bhubaneswar Chennai
Delhi Hyderabad Kolkata Lucknow Mumbai

Published by Jaico Publishing House
A-2 Jash Chambers, 7-A Sir Phirozshah Mehta Road
Fort, Mumbai - 400 001
jaicopub@jaicobooks.com
www.jaicobooks.com

PIT STOPS FOR PEAK PERFORMANCE
ISBN 978-81-8495-661-0

First Jaico Impression: 2015

Printed by

To the three women in my life

My mother Vimala Kantam – who shaped my values and taught me the passion for excellence

My mother in law Ratna Varadarajan – who taught me the importance of selfless service

My life partner Anuradha Rajan – my role model for inclusive leadership

ABOUT THE AUTHOR

Kanti Gopal Kovvali is the founder and CEO of a change management consultancy firm, Institution Builders HR Solutions Pvt Ltd (www.institutionbuilders.com). He is an OD specialist with significant expertise in large-scale change methodologies and building high performance work cultures.

Kathleen Dannemiller, a globally renowned exponent of large-scale change management, has trained Kanti. His expertise lies in simultaneously engaging hundreds of employees across an organization to build enthusiasm, positive restlessness and ownership for performance.

As part of Grow Talent Company, he popularized Career Transition support for down sized employees in India. The Gillette Career Transition project involving more than 200 people that he co-designed with the client and executed collaboratively won the DMA Erehwon award.

In the last twenty-two years, Kanti has provided consulting support to several leading multinational and Indian companies. As a change management consultant he has advised business leaders of companies such as IMRB International, Behr Engineering Services, SREI SAHAJ and Rane Limited. He has also been a visiting faculty in Tata Institute of Social Sciences (TISS) and Narsee Monjee Institute of Management Studies.

His professional thinking has been shaped by Jayaram Shetty of TISS, R C Sastry of VST Industries Limited, Sukumar of

Eicher Consultancy Services and Anil Sachdev of Grow Talent. The work of Medha Patkar and his TISS batch mates from social work influenced his activist thinking.

His deep passion for social change has led him to be associated with transformation work with community and education focused non-governmental organizations.

Apart from a state rank in intermediate and a university rank in graduation, Kanti has a postgraduate degree in HR from the Tata Institute of Social Sciences. Kanti Gopal is based in Navi Mumbai, India. He is married to Anuradha Rajan, an alumnus from TISS. Anuradha works on social change interventions. They have two teenage children. Kanti can be reached at kanti@ institutionbuilders.com

PREFACE

Do you chase high performance throughout the year?

Is this challenging?

Does it create high levels of stress in you?

In the last ten years of my consulting practice, I have worked with diverse organizations and hundreds of managers all of who are chasing high performance. Most of the managers take total accountability for their goals, identify opportunities and direct the energies of their team to achieve team goals. However, when I speak to such managers they sigh that it is becoming increasingly difficult to read the market, understand customer preferences, predict competitor moves, shape the organization's culture and be ready for the next disruptive change in their industry. At the same time, these managers accept these challenges as a way of life and put in greater effort year after year. After all, the purpose of any managerial role is to leverage opportunities, address constraints and achieve high organizational and team performance.

I assume that you are a high performing manager who aspires to be a celebrity CEO. Can you really sustain the pressure of chasing high performance year after year? We hear stories of so many people who burn out midway. Do you really want to continue to tread this path of chasing high performance? If there were indeed an alternative, would you like to explore?

In my consulting work, I came across several managers who seem to achieve high performances without any sweat. These managers seem to have all the time in the world to set new benchmarks and take up more challenges. While others get a "far exceeds performance rating" for some time and then burn out, these managers seem to go on and on forever.

I started researching these managers with the question "What do they do to achieve and sustain effortless high performance in an increasingly complex business and team environment?"

My research showed that these managers do something that is so commonsensical and obvious that it verges on the banal - they invest a lot of time in observing, reflecting and gaining insights – about their organization, their customers, their competitors, their team and each individual within it (including themselves).

When you are leading from the front and are totally immersed in task excellence, you may not really have time to reflect. If you do not reflect enough, you really cannot make the right decisions and course corrections. When you are surprised by the results of a customer feedback survey or employee satisfaction report or the sudden resignation of an employee or a change in market trends, you know that you have not invested enough in reflection at the right time. If you had done so, you would not have been taken by surprise.

This book is for managers who don't want to be caught unawares; who are open to the idea that they may need to change the lenses through which they view their managerial work. Once you change your lenses, you shift the energies from 'total action' to 'reflection-action-reflection'. In this book we explore the high leverage opportunities for managers to reflect and build capacities that make them and their team a winning combination.

This is not a theoretical book. It is an '**Apply as your read**' book.

However, there is a word of caution. You will benefit only if you get into the 'flow' of learning. Think of when we were at our learning best - when we were children. And why did we learn best as children? Why did we not become a prey to 'Why will it work' or 'What if it does not work' kind of mindset? This is because children refuse to be taken hostage by the mind. They learn the most as they are willing to suspend the cacophony of the rational mind and engage with new information in a non-judgmental way. They are not victims of assumptions and preconceived notions. For a moment, reflect on your childhood. As a child you just jumped into the water, experimented and learnt to swim. Are you willing to do the same by jumping into this book of learning, enjoy the process as it unfolds and achieve effortless high performance?

If so, step in and get set ...

Formula 1 Terminology used in this book

Lap: The distance travelled when driving around the Formula 1 circuit once.

Sector: For timing purposes each lap is split into three sections, each of which is roughly a third of the lap. These sections are officially known as Sector 1, Sector 2 and Sector 3.

This book is divided into Laps (Chapters). Each lap is further sub-divided into Sectors (sections). I have taken the poetic license to add more than three sectors in each lap of this book.

Contents

Lap 6
Mid year Appraisal Pit Stop

Lap 7
Self Pit Stop

Lap 8
Pause before the finish

Lap 9
Pit Stop Magic

Sector I

LAP 1
THE WINNING FORMULA

LAP 1 – SECTOR I

IN A RACE THAT IS BASED ON SPEED, WHAT DO YOU THINK DIFFERENTIATES THE WINNERS FROM OTHERS?

A re you a Formula 1 buff? Even if you are not, have you had a chance to watch a Formula 1 (F1) race? It is probably the most grueling race in the world. As you are aware, only the best qualify. These drivers are daredevils. They are physically fit and mentally tough. They are deeply passionate about the sport and have nerves of steel. They are backed by great machines, great automobile research and great support teams. There is nothing really that sets one F1 driver apart from the other among the top 10. If that is so, how is it that some of them win consistently? How are F1 drivers like Michael Schumacher in the past and Sebastian Vettel, Kimi Raikkonen, Lewis Hamilton and Mark Webber in the present so consistent in winning the race every time? What separates winners from those who "almost win"?

If this question bothers you, you will find this book interesting.

In a race where winning depends on speed and your ability to race ahead of others, what really differentiates winners from others are your SMART STOPS. This includes planned stops as well as unplanned stops. These stops in Formula 1 lingo are called PIT STOPS. Vehicles stop to fill in gas, change tires and handle minor or major repairs.

If winning is based solely on speed, you may wonder why not do away with the need for a pit stop. Put enough gas in the car for the race and have tires that do not wear out. Sure- it's possible. But this would make the vehicle bulky; the tires would have to be bigger and overall this might slow down the speed of the race car. On the other hand, if you stop for gas frequently, it could eat into the time that you gained otherwise. So what options do you really have, you might wonder. In reality, it is the pit stops in any race that can make or break a race. "A lot of races are won in the pit," according to IndyCar driver Will Power, "it is a team sport." (Rose 2011) Because of this, race teams plan a pit strategy before each race. This involves a schedule of planned pit stops that includes not only when they will take place during the course of the race, but also what services and adjustments will be performed at each stop. Let's see what exactly happens in a pit stop and what we can take back from this to our work as managers.

The ABC of a Pit Stop

In motorsports, a pit stop is where a racing vehicle stops in the Pit during a race for refueling, new tires, repairs, mechanical adjustments, a driver change, or any combination of the above.

The pit usually comprise of a pit lane which runs parallel to the start/finish straight and is connected at each end to the main track, and a row of garages (usually one per team) outside which the work is done.

Pit stop work is carried out by anywhere from five to twenty mechanics (also called a pit crew), depending on the series, while the driver waits in the vehicle (except where a driver change is involved).

In any race, pit strategy is one of the most important features of the race; this is because a racecar traveling at 100 miles per hour (160 kilometers per hour) will travel approximately 150 feet (45 meters) per second. During a ten-second pit stop, all of a car's competitors will gain approximately one-quarter of a mile (one-half kilometer) over the stopped car.

However, the car that made the additional pit stop will run faster on the race track than cars that did not make the stop, both because it can carry a smaller amount (and thus lower weight) of fuel, and will also have less wear on its tires, providing more traction and allowing higher speeds.

Source: Wikipedia

Because of this, race teams plan a pit strategy prior to the start of every race. There is a schedule for each car's planned pit stops during the race, and takes into account factors such as rate of fuel consumption, weight of fuel, cornering speed with each available tire compound, rate of tire wear, the effect of tire wear on cornering speed, the length of pit road and the track's pit road speed limit, and even expected changes in weather and lighting conditions.

STRATEGIZING A PIT STOP

While what is visible for all of us is the clockwork precision of the pit stops team, a lot of work happens behind the scenes. Pit stop teams train through the year. The manager, the driver, the pit stops crew make smart strategies for each race. This is because each track is different and hence the response of the driver and the team has to be specific. They visualize every possible situation that would require intervention. What if the track is wet? What if there is an oil spill on the track? What if there is some damage because of a brushing vehicle? What if a pit stop inadvertently went bad? What if … What if … Similarly after the race they hold an honest discussion about what we did well and what we need to do differently the next time around. All this together constitutes the pit stops strategy.

What's interesting here is the role each individual plays in making the pit stops strategy a success. While the driver is the visible face and is definitely a key contributor, one cannot underestimate the efforts of each member of the pit stops crew in contributing to a successful race.

Let's take McLaren Racing as an illustration. Since 1963, McLaren Racing has become one of the most successful and groundbreaking teams in Grand Prix motor racing, creating some of the most iconic Formula 1 cars in the sport's history. The team has won 4 consecutive Drivers' & Constructors' Championships ('88-'91), 8 Constructors' Championship titles and 12 Drivers' Championship titles.

However in April 2012, the team struggled in several grand prix due to a poor pit stops strategy, which caused their drivers – Jenson Button and Lewis Hamilton, crucial time loss, which eventually resulted in low scores. Jenson Button's hopes of victory in China were wrecked by a slow stop and later teammate Lewis Hamilton also faced two agonizing delays. Lewis Hamilton, the 2008 F1 champion, who also lost time in Malaysia in the pit, ended the Bahrain Grand Prix in eighth place and lost the lead in the overall standings to Red Bull's winner and world champion Sebastian Vettel.

In June 2012 European Grand Prix a failed front jack cost Lewis Hamilton second place and possibly even the race. A failure of McLaren's new front wheel jack meant a second jack had to be found in order to complete the stop. Sam Michael, McLaren's sporting director, felt the heat as McLaren struggled with glaring fumbles during their pit stops.

BETTERING THE PIT STOPS

In June 2012, McLaren carried out a thorough investigation of their pit stops procedures, after suffering costly holdups during the Bahrain Grand Prix, for the third successive race.

"Pit stops are definitely better now," said Michael. "What we've done is work a lot on equipment, and also the people. We brought a lot of things like retained wheel nuts, quick release jacks, a traffic light system, so really for McLaren for the whole lot we've been on an upward curve on equipment to get it right. We've changed a lot of people around as well. We've been fixed now for the last three races."

THE TURNAROUND

In July 2012 the McLaren pit crew delivered a smart 2.5 seconds tire change, which allowed Jenson Button to peel into second place (ahead of Red Bull's F1 driving ace Sebastian Vettel) after the final stop. Jenson Button's car rolled into the pit box and 24 mechanics sprinted out of the garage as his £1.5million cutting-edge F1 car was hoisted into the air. "Less than three seconds later it was pulling away having had a complete tire change on all four wheels" said Michael. (*Source*: **YallaF1.com**)

Most people would feel that cars that stop many times during a race for a quick maintenance check or change of tires would invariably loose- because these pit stops are a waste of time. But this is far from the truth. The reason is that these stops are critical in making the car more efficient. For example, research shows that increased speed resulting from change in tires helps race cars reach the end line a second earlier.

Imagine a car making three stops over the course of a race to change tires, taking a total of 90 seconds. Your fresher tires then get you to the chequered flag 91 seconds before you otherwise would have. Despite stopping three times, you've reached the finish line one second earlier, potentially pipping your rivals to glory.

Isn't your work like the Formula 1 race where you are racing for excellence through the year? To move faster than others, the ideal approach is to make a business strategy for the next 2-5 years and get every one into high-speed action. Even if you plan diligently and have a well thought out strategy blue print, constant changes in the external environment and changes within your organization may not let you succeed. You need pit stops to reflect, change and move ahead. The quantities as well as the quality of your pit stops position you for success or failure.

If pit stops differentiate the winners from others ... please reflect if you plan for enough pit stops in a year? If indeed you do so, how **smart are your pit stops?**

Please pause and reflect before you continue reading.

LAP 1– SECTOR II

SHOULD PIT STOPS MATTER FOR ORGANIZATIONS, TEAMS AND MANAGERS?

Are pit stops really a big deal for an organization? Think of the goals of 2013-14 that you as a leader set for the organization or your department or your team. Were they easy to achieve? They may not really be. In today's world no company sets easy goals. If your organization had challenging goals, it necessarily means that your department, team and individual members had high stretch goals. Let's say somehow you managed to achieve this year's goals and better still exceeded them. Can you take a break? The answer would be Sorry, no! The goals for 2014-15 are probably going to be tougher. Maybe 25-50% higher than what you struggled to achieve in the last 12 months. In all probability, the resources would remain the same or less, the capabilities of team members would not dramatically change from what they were on March 31st to the 1st of April. You cannot even go slow for a few months and then take off. The monthly goals will simply start piling up.

So what will you do to achieve the goals? After all your company's future and your career are at stake. Maybe if you are a smart leader, you will manage the situation by controlling it tightly - tell people what to do, keep the pressure on your team, conduct more meetings etc. However, this may not be sustainable.

Importantly, if you become so pre-occupied with your team's work by getting hands on, can you effectively do the real work for which you have been hired? At the same time the reality is if you trust and delegate and god forbid they do not achieve their goals, your future is at stake.

This is where PIT STOPS can come to your rescue!

The only way you can achieve higher goals for your organization, team and self is through new ideas, break through thinking, tapping unrealized potential and addressing bad habits. Can you do all this when people are in action? You need to create time to reflect, ideate and get charged. You need to pause. You need a PIT STOP or may be several pit stops because action and reflection can seldom happen together.

Maybe organization level pit stops make sense. But should you be bothered about individual pit stops with your team members?

Imagine a Formula race in motion. You are the driver. You are agile and are skillfully dodging opponents and moving forward. However, you are facing challenges in overtaking them. Let's say that your coach is giving a running commentary on the wireless – at times appreciating, at times expressing disappointment, at times telling you what to do - back seat driving at its best. Can you concentrate on the race, listen to the advice, reflect on changes that are required and implement them simultaneously?

But isn't this exactly how many managers behave? Try to manage high performance by continuous interference? If someone were to do this to you, wouldn't this unsettle you? How can a team member perform at his best if he feels that he is being constantly evaluated?

When a person is performing at his best, there is an unconscious synchronicity between thought and action, - in other words, the person is in "full flow". In this state performance happens effortlessly. When a manager interrupts the team member constantly, the person becomes conscious and tentative. Now he is no longer performing, he is just waiting to be interrupted.

The role of a manager is to enable his team members to bring out the best of who he/she is. Constant interference, advising and feedback do not help. A manager needs to call for a time off, just like they do in sports, and use the time off period for feedback and reflection. This is the reason why pit stops are crucial in the first place. Pit stops can be effective when you, as a manager, ask questions that challenge assumptions, generates new ideas through which the road ahead seems smoother.

However, if the pit stop is conducted in a lousy manner, it only leads to a decline in performance. Managers who through their body language or direct communication make team members feel stupid, inadequate and helpless during the pit stops should be prepared that their team member's performance will go down further after the pit stops.

Do Team Pit Stops Really Matter?

If a manager conducts effective pit stops with each of his team members, should it not be sufficient? Is it really necessary for the manager to conduct a team pit stop? Well it is and for several reasons.

The construct of any organization is based on the notion of inter-dependence and hence the need to collaborate. As a manager, participating in a team pit stop and watching the interactions between team members gives you a good sense of how well the team is combining with each other to create value. It also helps you to gain insights into where you need to invest your managerial time to bring in greater team synergies.

What do individual members miss if there are no team pit stops? Team pit stops are learning opportunities to discover, utilize and build on each other's strengths and ideas. Team pit stops build a sense of common identity, a feeling of a community and determination not to let down others.

Do you need Self Pit Stops?

I would say a resounding yes! To become successful, managers, need to identify their strengths and hone them. This happens when they plan pit stops for themselves. Deliberate practice converts the strengths into competences. However, anything that you develop to a level of excellence generates a flip side. For example, if you become an excellent planner, you may find difficulty in handling fuzzy situations.

If you are great at inter-personal relations, you may struggle with being task focused. Self pit stops help successful managers to not only remind themselves of their strengths but also reflect on how to neutralize the side effects (flip side) of their strengths.

LAP 1 – SECTOR III

ARE YOU PIT STOPS PHOBIC?

Do you conduct pit stops? While for many this may look like a non-question, we have come across several heroic leaders and managers who do not believe in pit stops. In many organizations managers do not conduct feedback sessions with their employees. Several of them skip face to face annual appraisal meetings with their team members. Some managers prefer seeking ideas through emails rather than holding a team meeting and discussing an issue threadbare. Managers rarely hold pit stops with employees to seek ideas on market trends and strategy. In many organizations, annual planning and review pit stops do not happen until almost three months into the financial year. One cannot but wonder if managers are pit stops phobic.

In my experience I have found the following pit stops are strategic for every kind of organization.

Business Planning and Review	Innovation	Supplier Feedback	Project Team Review
Budget Planning and Review	Customer Feedback	Regular Department and Team Review	Individual Goal Setting and Review

These are pit stops that can be planned in advance. We are going to refer to them as *planned pit stops*. Let's understand each of these pit stops in detail.

BUSINESS PLANNING AND REVIEW PIT STOPS

Many companies mistake this pit stop for an annual budget planning and review pit stops. Business planning and business reviews are about long-term strategy. The definition of long term could vary from industry to industry. This could mean anywhere from a year from now to 10 years from now. Business planning is akin to how the drivers and their constructors prepare for the entire F1 season. The F1 season consists of a series of races, known as Grand Prix (from French, originally meaning great prizes), held throughout the world on purpose-built circuits and public roads. The results of each race are evaluated using a points system to determine two annual World Championships, one for the drivers and one for the constructors.

The objective of the business planning and review pit stops should be to deliberate on trends, visualize scenarios and think through the preparedness of the company to handle each of the scenarios. It should be a comprehensive process engaging people from across different levels in the organization as well as key external stakeholders such as customers, suppliers, industry experts and relevant others. In fact, this is a fundamental requirement for strategic planning. Effective strategies have to be evolved systemically, by looking at backward and forward linkages, by identifying known and unknown variables. This cannot happen if business planning is limited to a handful of people in the higher echelons of the company.

BUDGET PLANNING AND REVIEW PIT STOPS

This pit stop is an opportunity to deliberate and come up with innovative ideas on how to accelerate implementation of strategy. This is akin to what each of the F1 teams do before any race. They think through afresh on the race strategy based on conditions, competition and leveraging a racer's strengths.

While this is a significant pit stop, have you experienced in your organization the farcical drama of this pit stop using 'excel' formulas? Microsoft's Excel comes in handy for doing all the shady work. Excel is used as a tool to juggle and re-juggle numbers so that they become acceptable to the top management. Actually these numbers mean nothing to anyone. They only ensure false comfort. The numbers help managers fool each other in a meeting effortlessly.

INNOVATION PIT STOPS

What could the future look like? What could be the possible scenarios? Imagining the future helps an organization not only to be prepared to face it but also to shape it wherever possible. This pit stop is the mother of all pit stops. In order for this pit stop to be effective you need to engage with diverse people within your organization and also outside your organization.

In many organizations people who participate in this pit stop are of similar level or of similar background. Hence they tend to conform to similar assumptions and lines of thinking.

CUSTOMER AND SUPPLIER FEEDBACK PIT STOPS

Whether one wants it or not customers give feedback. I suppose it is their habit. Generally feedback flows more heavily when they feel outraged. Sometimes feedback is also given when the company has done a good job. Sometimes it is verbal. Sometimes it is written. Sometimes it is through a survey. Customer feedback pit stops are those where you reflect on the spontaneous and not so spontaneous feedback of customers to improve your products and services.

In the course of my consulting assignments on building customer centric cultures, I have interviewed scores of people across different levels on whether they knew that their company had conducted a customer feedback survey. If yes, what does the customer say about the company's products and services? In my experience approximately only 70% of the employees knew about the survey and only 20% of them actually knew what the customer had said. In a few companies the feedback results were shared as a communication exercise. However, this is not equivalent to a pit stop. Pit stops are deliberate reflection events.

For example, pit stops conducted after customer surveys should include employees across different levels in the organization. These pit stops should be used to analyse the numbers generated by the survey, using the employees' own stories and experiences. That is adding 'flesh and blood' to the numbers, rather than using numbers alone as the basis for interpreting the survey results. By not conducting serious pit stops to reflect and act on customer feedback, companies lose the opportunity to transform their business model and organizational way of working.

In more than one management meeting, I have heard senior leader's talk of suppliers as necessary evils who need to be managed. Suppliers are seen as a cost and as a drain, not as a source of creativity and partnership. Generally suppliers who work with such companies reciprocate the attitude of the company. After all you get back what you give. Properly handled supplier pit stops are opportunities to get ideas and commitment to make your customers successful.

PROJECT REVIEWS PIT STOPS

Organizations often set up cross functional projects. These are aimed at addressing critical issues that need collective thinking and collaboration of different departments. Members who are nominated into such teams belong to different departments. Apart from contributing to the project, they also generally handle their regular departmental duties. Such project teams meet regularly, ideate, review progress and take decisions to ensure project effectiveness.

Each project review meeting is a pit stop. But they can be effective only when there are honest conversations between team members; they are accountable to each other and demonstrate a sense of urgency to achieve the project mandate successfully. However, more often than not, the structure to manage such projects poses serious challenges in making the project review an effective pit stops. This is because each member reports to and is evaluated by their department head and hence the project remains a priority only if the department head deems so. If the department head is not convinced about the value of such projects, it gets pushed way down on the list of priorities for the team member reporting to him. Thus project team members may find themselves challenged by conflicting priorities and loyalties. In such a situation, projects are plagued by delays and become ineffective; project review meetings become slinging matches where blame games, lame excuses for delays and a general lack of commitment prevent these spaces from being effective pit stops.

REGULAR DEPARTMENT, TEAM AND INDIVIDUAL GOAL SETTING AND REVIEW PIT STOPS

These pit stops are basic for effective working - whether this is at the level of a department, work team or an individual. Taking a pause to reflect is a minimum condition for effective routine management. No one would dispute this premise and to be fair these pit stops happen quite often. However, the quality of these pit stops is where there might be a problem. This is because this pit stop is not seen as a seamless part of continuous improvement. Instead, it is considered an unavoidable pain that needs to be managed and gotten over with.

Do you have these pit stops in your organization? If you do, are you sure these pit stops are being used really well?

Please pause and reflect before you continue reading.

I want to share with you examples of effective planned pit stops adopted by various organizations. Under each example I have shared my perspective about the pit stops in italics, what organizations can learn from it and how to make the pit stops more effective.

MARRIOTT HOTELS: 'DAILY PACKET' PIT STOP

Marriott has a daily newsletter called the Daily Packet. This is read at the beginning of the day in each of their hotels. The Daily Packet is a communication tool that comprises of the hospitality basic of the day, events for the day, daily birthdays, special guest recognition of associate efforts, HR eye opener for the day, Employee anniversaries, welcome note for new employees etc.

A key part of the daily packet is the Daily Basic – this is the behavior for the day that Marriott employees are supposed to practice. It also has all relevant information about the business of that hotel property for the previous day like occupancy rate, key customer complaints and suggestions.

Let's see what makes this a great pit stop.

Many organisations do not share their business information on a daily basis with their employees. This stems from two assumptions- one that employees cannot be trusted with this information and two that they are not capable of using this information. However, by doing this, employees are seldom able to see the larger picture. They are unable to connect what they are doing with what the company requires.

When people have the overall perspective of how the business is doing, what customers are saying, they become savvy and are able to align their role and goals to what is important for the organization. Marriot's 'daily packet' pit stop treats employees as adults and gives them respect. It is data based and shared with every employee. It fosters ownership. Celebrating employees and discussing problems honestly promotes a community feeling. Therein lies the value of Marriott's daily packet - building trust to achieve high performance. A great pit stop indeed!

INNOVATION JAM PIT STOP OF IBM:

Can the top management team of a large global organization such as IBM provide leadership in terms of setting the growth and direction of their subsidiaries, sitting at their headquarters? They tried doing this and found it was not working. This is when they started an interesting process in 2001, using their intranet platform. They titled it as World Jam. Jamming is defined by Oxford Dictionary as something that is informal and involves everyone. IBM adopted this model and involved all their employees, across the globe, in brainstorming for ideas. On their intranet they put up specific burning questions that needed smart solutions. They asked their employees to pause, reflect and think of innovative solutions to problems plaguing the company. For example, an issue being faced by the company was on how to build high speed machines without compromising on quality. Over a period of three days IBMers shared thousands of ideas. People built on each other's ideas. What came out of the process was amazing and they managed to find the most effective solution to marry speed and quality. This pit stop worked because of active leadership, concrete outputs and total ownership for implementing the ideas that emerged from the process, from thousands of IBMers across the globe.

IBM realized the power of engaging employees in substantial conversations. Jamming has now become part of IBM's culture. In one of the Jams on innovation, their CEO at that time, Sam Palmisano, pledged $100 million for the best ideas and ultimately funded 10 of the 37,000 submitted, including five new businesses.

WHAT MADE THIS PIT STOP WORK?

World Jam as a philosophy involves everyone and encourages building on ideas. It enables confluence of different perspectives and makes ideas stronger. As a method it is time bound, topics are specific and it is easy to use. Respect for everyone's ideas, fairness in processing the data (building on ideas, multi voting) and honest agenda (issues that are critical for the organization's success) makes this a great pit stop.

Let's say, you are excited with this process. However, your organization is not tech savvy. You can still conduct the jamming process location wise. Here's one way it could be done - within your location, identify a room or a corridor. Paste brown paper on the walls. Prominently display the topic on which you would like group brainstorming. Keep post-its and pencils next to the brown paper. Set aside one hour in the morning and one hour in the evening aside as brainstorming hours. During this time employees can come individually or in groups, think through ideas, write them on the Post-it along with their name and paste them on the brown sheets. Give three days for this brainstorming exercise. After that, involve a group of volunteers to do an affinity of the ideas. Put up the affinity list and conduct multi voting. The shortlisted ideas can be taken up for acting upon. One question you may have is the extent to which we go by the collective wisdom of the group. Shouldn't experts vet the ideas? Your anxiety is reasonable but research done in recent times indicates the value of collective wisdom over expert advice.

CONNECT + DEVELOP PIT STOP OF P & G

If you are the owner or the manager of a small or medium company I am sure you have often thought that if only you were a lot bigger, you would have spent significantly more on research and development. Let's say 'abracadabra' you one day actually become a large global conglomerate. Now you have the money to invest in serious R&D. Will you be content with innovations flowing from your own R&D department? What is your guess?

If you are P&G, you will be extremely dissatisfied. So much so that Langley, who was their CEO during the last decade, decided to invite outside developers to participate in P&G's innovation efforts and contribute to new products and product components. This was met with much skepticism from those within the company. After all, how could outsiders know the business, products and customers better than company experts? Could they be trusted? What was it that external experts could bring into R&D that company scientists didn't already know? But the CEO decided that seeking ideas from outsiders such as consultants would make the R&D more robust. And this strategy worked. As the concept started to yield results, skepticism inside the company converted to evangelism. P&G introduced Connect + Develop program. This pit stop allows outside developers to get their concepts and designs into P&G's product pipeline. An applicator developed by Cardinal Health (now Catalent), for example, helped P&G launch Olay Regenerist Eye Derma-Pods, now its top-selling skin-care item.

As you become successful, you develop strong views about what to innovate, where to innovate and how to innovate. Many times these actually turn into blinkers and limit your thinking. This is natural. The very same products and innovations which helped you become successful in the past may come in the way of identifying other potential opportunities. An 'outsider' does not have these constraints. He/ She may obviously have other blinkers. Nevertheless your baggage will not condition them and if you are willing to listen, engage, collaborate and experiment you can get amazing results. The success of this pit stop lies in respecting each other, caring for each other's interests and building trusting relations.

If P&G can do this, so can you. If your company is an SME (Small or Medium Enterprise) and you are competing against large companies, such a pit stop will create a level playing field for innovation and growth.

'Do you dare to dream?' Pit Stop at Danone

How often do you spend time dreaming about the future? How often do you imagine yourself as Superman or Superwoman with the holy mandate to change the world? All of us do, sometimes in hope and sometimes in despair. Danone UK channelizes this restlessness in each of us through a program called "Do you dare to dream?"

Every year, Danone gives every employee a "dream cloud," a piece of paper on which they can write out their dream. The only stipulation is that the dream should be possible for the company to make it happen. The paper is then posted on a "dream board," displayed in the office for everyone to see. After four weeks, everyone votes on which dream they would like to see come true. The company fully funds the dream of the person who receives the most votes. Through this program, one person cycled the entire length of Great Britain to raise money for a children's hospice; another undertook a two-month pilgrimage from France to Spain; another returned to Vietnam to find her birth mother, and another went to Cape Town, South Africa to build a house in his native township through Habitat for Humanity.

People get into an auto mode in organizations. The "Do you dare to dream" program is an interesting way to wake up people, get them to become childlike and dream about the possibility to make a difference to the world. This is a great pit stop to evoke the spirit of giving back to the community and doing things beyond personal gratification. By doing this employees are able to connect with a higher purpose and this positivity is most likely to spill over into their work.

My recommendation to Danone UK is that it could derive greater value from this pit stop if it extends the Dare to Dream approach to seek ideas for growing the organization.

How did you find the pit stops that you just read about? Were they interesting? Did they provoke you to think?

Pause and think about whether your organization has a culture of reflection? Or are you an organization, which thrives on constant action and doing?

If your answer is no to the first question and yes to the second, you might need to work on building a culture of reflection and analysis in your organization or, a culture of PIT STOPS!

However, if you have a PIT STOPS culture, reflect on how well are you leveraging those pit stops?

Given below is a set of markers that will help you assess how effective your pit stops currently are.

PIT STOPS EFFECTIVENESS MONITOR

Reflect on the statements given below. If you and your team members' answer to each of these statements is an emphatic **YES**, then your planned pit stops are effective.

1. We look forward to our pit stops.

2. We plan our pit stops, circulate the agenda and prepare for pit stops discussions.

3. We are on time for the pit stops meetings and in general do justice to all agenda items.

4. We involve all relevant stakeholders. They include people at various levels, from various departments and even those who are external to our organization.

5. Everyone gets a fair hearing during pit stops discussions. Sufficient time is spent on getting divergent views.

6. The pit stops discussion is data based and decisions are based on 'what is said' rather than 'who said it'.

7. The discussion is aimed at ensuring convergence of the entire team on the final decision.

8. People are honest in sharing their feelings and perspectives.

9. At the end of pit stop discussions, all the team members feel energized; leave the room with a clear direction and feel committed to the decisions taken.

LAP 1 – SECTOR IV

DO YOU PLAN FOR PIT STOPS TO HANDLE AN OUT OF ORDINARY SITUATION?

Unplanned Pit Stops

There are events that you do not anticipate, those where you are taken by surprise. In such cases you cannot plan the pit stops in advance. This is something like the race-car skidding and damaging its tire due to an oil spill on the track. Such a situation needs an unplanned pit stop. Even in business and within your team you may face the need for unplanned pit stops. Do you schedule such pit stops when needed and do it without delay? If you do, do you know if they are effective?

I want to now introduce you to unplanned pit stops that many companies have to make. As you read, reflect on your own unplanned pit stops and how effective they are.

Examples of Effective Unplanned Pit Stops

Supreme Court of FedEx Pit Stop

Let's say that a decision has been taken concerning an employee that he/ she is terribly unhappy about. What can that employee do? Who can the person talk to? Maybe his boss; maybe HR.

But what if the boss has been the one to take the decision? Maybe the person can talk to his/ her boss's boss. What if the

CEO of the company has taken the decision? Well then, its either my way or the high way.

In most companies this is how the story ends.

However, there are some companies where it doesn't quite end this way. FedEx set up the "Supreme Court of FedEx" as a redress for employee grievances. The interesting feature is that this "Supreme Court" can overrule even the FedEx CEO's decisions. You may wonder whether setting up such a supra structure has created chaos and undermined the CEO's authority? The answer is no. On the contrary, it has brought in greater accountability in taking fair decisions. FEDEX's own assumption behind setting up such as mechanism was that in most cases people act responsibly when given authority. The trust inherent in such a move has also meant that employees have not misused this. It has strengthened trusting relations between employees and the company.

This system provides excellent opportunities for an unplanned pit stop for employee issues. What it does is to legitimize employees' requests for immediate senior management attention. The normal hierarchy does not allow for such speed or undiluted presentation of issues to the management.

However, there is a possibility for leveraging this platform even more effectively if it is used to highlight strategic and operational issues as well.

Grievance Hotline Pit Stop of Honeywell

As a Honeywell employee, if you are unhappy about a particular policy, practice or action and want to highlight them anonymously, you can use the online tool to record your grievance. The same will be delivered to the mailboxes of the Head of HR and the Manager HR.

There is an obligation on these individuals to look into the grievance and take appropriate action. The status of each grievance needs to be updated regularly to help the employee track the progress of the grievance logged in by him/ her.

This grievance redress mechanism is like a red flag for the company's management - a significant pit stop because it highlights rumbling discontent that may affect performance, employee engagement and attrition. The paradigm governing this practice is that management should be alerted about simmering discontent early on, especially in organizations which are highly action driven.

My opinion is that this hotline can also be used as a powerful pit stop for highlighting business threats, opportunities or innovative ideas directly with the leadership team.

In organizations, we invest a lot of time to help people become effective race track drivers. Do we invest time on how to reflect and manage pit stops effectively? Are we missing the essence of what truly contributes to business success? Are we underestimating the power of individual and group reflection? I have not seen too many organizations invest in training workshops on how to reflect or on how to participate in meetings effectively or on how to conduct meetings effectively. If the organizational construct is based on collaboration and organizational contexts keep changing all the time, SMART pit stops guarantee that an organization does not lose its plot midway.

Epilogue: The Curious Case of an Effective Unplanned Pit Stop that turned Ineffective Midway

As I end this section, I want to introduce you to an interesting real case of an effective pit stop that turned ineffective midway.

A construction company engaged me recently to help them facilitate a three-day pit stop dialogue. The company was not doing well and was at the verge of receiving a financial rescue package from a bank. In this context the pit stop was a crucial one for building a sense of urgency, ownership and accountability. All senior leaders, project managers and service department heads were to participate in this pit stop dialogue.

My engagement with the company began a month before the pit stop. A cross section of participants including the senior leaders were involved in designing the three day pit stop.

They found the process of designing and preparing for the pit stop transformational. There were honest conversations, some heartburn and a great many collaborative actions.

The D-day was around the corner when the owner of the company threw a spanner in the works. With just a day left before the pit stop was to take place, he introduced a new CEO! Until then, the owner was doubling up as the CEO. The new CEO wanted to prove his worth from the word go. And he chose to do this by questioning the entire design of the pit stop. When he found that he was not able to make any significant alterations, he announced that the entire meeting design (meant for three days) should be packed into two days as he needed the third day for presentations by senior leaders in the organization. He positioned these presentations as important for the project managers as they needed to know the business strategy and improvement plans. Everyone could sense that the new CEO had a hidden agenda but no one was in a position to call his bluff.

The first two days went off extremely well. As the process was highly participatory, it generated a tremendous sense of ownership. Videos showing customer and banker expectations created a positive restlessness among employees. The root cause analysis sessions brought forth specific and measurable issues that needed to be addressed. The second day ended with a whole group commitment to turn around the company. The new CEO was watching and waiting.

The third day began with presentations, just as the new CEO wanted. The first presentation was by a senior leader who was respected across the company. The new CEO challenged his financial data rather aggressively. There was pin drop silence in the hall containing more than 200 people, as the CEO sharply tore into what had been presented. People saw the drama unfold as the new CEO started using rude language and insulted the entire team for non-performance. What the new CEO said was not wrong, but what people in the room including me, could remember was only how he said it. The euphoria of the first two days ended there.

At the end of the third day people left the room feeling vulnerable. Maybe they were a non-performing group, but how could one say with certainty if the company's current financial state was only because of 200 under performers in the room or because of an underperforming owner? Even if they were the cause, how would making them feel stupid achieve the objective of the pit stop? How can 200 people who felt incapable take capable decisions in the future?

Please pause and reflect on how effective are your unplanned pit stops, using the two questions given below:

1. How much lead-time does it require for your organization or your team to hold an unplanned pit stop?

2. Does your organization or your team perform better or "take off" after the unplanned pit stop or does it slide backwards?

LAP 2

THE SOUL OF A PIT STOP

LAP 2 – SECTOR I

WHY SHOULD YOUR TEAM CARE ABOUT YOUR PIT STOP SUCCESS?

Is handling a pit stop just about a technique? Is it just about using some tools and methods at the appropriate time? If yes, it should not matter who is conducting the pit stop. If the technique is right, the results should be good. But in the process of working with organizations on managing change, I have learnt that the character of the person conducting the pit stop is probably more important than mastery over the technique of running a pit stop. I have found in my experience that team members are forgiving about poor skills in running such pit stops but they do not take poor character kindly. If your team members are suspicious about your intent in holding such a meeting, even the savviest facilitation may not be enough in making the pit stop effective. Trust often overrides the correctness of the skill.

How do you know if you have the character that contributes to an effective pit stop? Your honest answer to this simple question will let you know this.

If your team members had a choice, would they still choose you as their manager?

If yes, then you are their Leader of Choice and your pit stops are likely to be high acceleration opportunities. If you are not your team's leader of choice, however skilled you are at facilitating pit stops, people will not buy into what you are saying or doing. Your pit stops are likely to be unmitigated disasters.

My extensive consulting practice with managers and their teams has helped me evolve a model for becoming a Leader of Choice and leverage the pit stops. I call this the 'Trust-Performance Model'.

EXPLAINING THE TRUST-PERFORMANCE MODEL

In general, good managers understand the value of pit stops. Hence they try to leverage the power of the pit stop by focusing on the three contributors of a high performance pit stop:

1. Plan and execute

2. Learn and review

3. Grow team and individual potential

Thoughtful planning and focused execution gives rise to a sense of contribution among individuals in the team. Review and learning accelerates performance. Growth uncovers hidden potential.

However, let's say you do not trust this skilled manager. Will these three contributors matter now? Maybe or maybe not; As an employee, you may have a niggling suspicion regarding the intention of the person and so may not be able to engage fully. If you are in the unfortunate position of being the manager who is not trusted, the sense of distrust among your team members can bring down your skills to zero.

How then can you build trust?

There are three elements that build trust. These are respect, fairness and authenticity.

1. Respect is differentiating the person from the individual's performance. You always respect the person though you may be critical of the individual's performance. Very often as managers we land up providing feed-back in a way where what we are saying is lost in how we are saying it.

2. Fairness is objectivity. It is managing people by using data, not notions or past experiences or hearsay.

3. Authenticity is tough love. A manager is authentic when she cares and hence spells out the truth – good or bad. Authenticity shines through when one doesn't judge people but their actions.

When a manager consistently demonstrates respect, fairness and authenticity, the person creates what can be called, "the smell of the place". Just like you can sniff good or bad odor and do not need to be told by others about odor (unless you have a bad cold), you can sniff the cultural odor of a workplace. Respect, fairness and authenticity create a cultural odor that attracts people and makes you the leader of their choice.

However, having said that, trust, a key contributor to the smell of the place does not automatically lead to effortless high performance. It only makes it easier. When managers build trust and leverage it for high performance they become Leaders of Choice and their pit stops become high leverage opportunities.

Leader of Choice Model

Build Trust – Build Performance

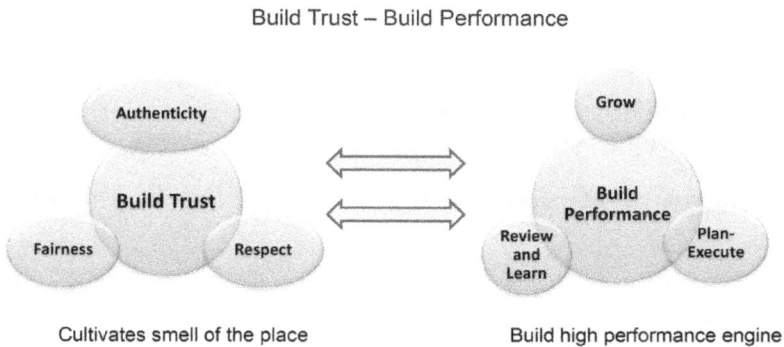

Cultivates smell of the place   Build high performance engine

How can you begin this journey of practicing the Trust Performance Model, becoming a leader of choice and leveraging your pit stops? There are different ways to do it. You can either live the model in entirety or   do so in stages. If you choose the second option, here's how you can go about it stage by stage.

SUPPORTIVE LEADER

- The first stage is to become a 'Supportive Leader'. Members under a supportive leader feel respected and they see a method to the work that they are doing. Careful planning and focused execution make members feel good about what they have done at the end of the day. In such a team you find no evidence of fire fighting or very less prevalence of it. Effective team planning and team review pit stops are the hallmark of a supportive manager.

Respect	Careful Planning and Execution
Intangible ⟶	**Tangible**

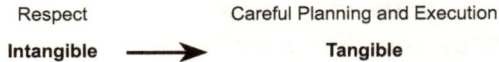

Leaders who are Supportive Managers get good employee engagement scores. Work life balance is in abundance. You can see the joy of working on the team members' faces.

When you hear of these work practices in a team, you can safely assume that their team manager is a Supportive Manager.

1. *Celebrating personal and professional successes of team members.*

2. *Factoring the personal aspirations as well as challenges of team members in work allocation and ensuring work flexibility.*

3. *Empathetic listening to grievances as well as ideas of team members.*

4. *Acceptance of individual idiosyncrasies and personal choices.*

Performance Leader

• The second stage is to become a 'Performance Leader'. Members under a performance leader feel valued and experience equity. Equity refers to the quality of being even and just, rewarding talent based on merit. There is a sense of objectivity. There are continuous reviews and these forums are used for accelerating learning rather than fixing blame. People come out of review sessions energized and hungry to set new performance benchmarks.

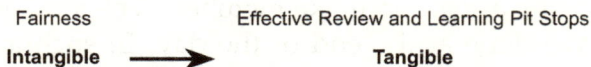

Fairness	Effective Review and Learning Pit Stops
Intangible ⟶	**Tangible**

Leaders who are Performance Managers know how to convert the potential in their team members to high performance. Such

Managers can handle tough conversations especially during appraisals. Their team members are celebrated across the unit as high performers.

Indicative work practices in a Performance Manager's team include

1. *Spontaneous performance feedback*

2. *Sharing role expectations periodically*

3. *Regular structured performance feedback*

4. *Peer to peer capability building*

5. *Celebrating Good Work (not just any work)*

GROWTH LEADER

- The third stage is to become a 'Growth leader'. Members under a growth leader experience their team as a family where all members are treated as equals. You are not a resource; you are the soul of the team. Conversations are honest and relationships are deep. The team is not a junction for taking another train. It is in fact the destination. Managers help members to discover their potential and help them to grow. They are willing to let go members to other teams if it helps them in their growth.

Authenticity   Pit Stops to Grow Hidden Potential

Intangible ⟶ **Tangible**

Leaders who are Growth leaders build their work teams into a community. They instill the spirit of being a 'tribe'. They challenge team and individual limitations. They exhort members to use their strengths to the fullest. They expand the boundaries of individual and team performance. They grow the organization and also build capabilities within the team to manage organizational growth. In effect, they build future leaders. While Performance Managers increase the individual and team's current capabilities, Growth Leaders enhance the potential of individuals and teams, which is futuristic. Members stay and work with such leaders for a very long time.

When you find a manager who promotes practices such as these, you can be sure that the person is a Growth Leader

1. *Team rituals that foster a sense of community. These include joining rituals, induction rituals and non-negotiable values.*

2. *Only those high performances which are achieved by following non-negotiable values are celebrated in the team. Any compromise in values is not tolerated and people found breaking them do not last long in the team.*

3. *Members routinely break their role boundaries to help each other succeed.*

4. *'We' language in ideation, planning and implementation.*

Each stage is an evolution towards becoming a Leader of Choice. One without the other is meaningless. However, if you want to take the first step, become a supportive leader, then a performance leader and then a growth leader. Together it builds your leadership brand and makes your team confer upon you the tag of the Leader of Choice. When you are the leader of choice people trust you, they trust your pit stops. Trust, when leveraged is what leads to high performance.

THE BUTTERFLY EFFECT OF BUILDING TRUST

Edward Lorenz coined the term 'Butterfly Effect' to illustrate how a butterfly flapping its wings in a distant place can cause a hurricane formation. Even those who find the flap-hurricane connection outrageous will appreciate the power of small insignificant events, in causing far-reaching changes. Small actions of managers towards their team members build enduring loyalties or evoke virulent bitterness. Pit stops that involve review or ideation or learning require members to be comfortable being vulnerable. This can only happen when they trust their managers. Managers cannot build trust in an instant. They need to demonstrate respect, fairness and authenticity consistently and in full measure throughout the year. Simple behaviors of managers such as greeting people, being attentive to members' grievances, genuinely listening to ideas and celebrating their presence create small un-noticeable changes in the team member's perception of the manager. Before one realizes, the manager exhibiting such seemingly simple actions accumulates abundant trust and becomes the leader of choice. Trust powers organizational, team and individual pit stops. Effective pit stops result in excellent performance. And this is what differentiates winners from others.

LAP 2 – SECTOR II

PRACTICES AND TOOLS THAT MAKE YOU A LEADER OF CHOICE

Some Interesting Practices that you can use to elevate yourself from a mere leader to a leader of choice:

1. *Build camaraderie:* One way to do this may be to start a Facebook account for your team. People can put up photographs, share personal and professional dimensions of their work or any other details which make them who they are. This works very well if the team does not meet too often or is spread across various locations. Such a Facebook account opens team members to the lives of each other and builds camaraderie. Once this takes off, do not be content with personal bonding. Elevate the relationship by engaging them to think business. Ask questions that make people think of innovative business and departmental strategies and that challenge their assumptions.

2. *Look for ways to deepen engagement among team members:* An example of this is to create a rotating role titled 'Life Coach', within the team. People double up to perform this role along with their regular work responsibilities. As a part of this role the life coach helps members to balance their personal and professional priorities, focus on aspirations, helps them to surface and resolve conflicts etc. As a life coach, members learn to empathize and connect with their team members at a deeper level. Do not worry too much about the title 'life coach'. While it sounds heavy, people quickly learn and define the role in their own way. It is essentially a way to get team members help each other.

3. *Truth and reconciliation (with due credit to Nelson Mandela):* Design forums where angst is voiced, heard and healed. For instance, create a Friday baggage forum wherein people can share things that caused them unhappiness during the week working with each other or in the team. Getting the baggage out of the system helps in coming in lightweight on Monday. It also helps you to address the causes of unhappiness. But a word of caution here – very often these forums can turn into acrimonious pit to level personal scores. To ensure this does

not happen, set some basic rules - the feedback should be data driven and team members should focus on how/what they felt rather than what the other person did.

4. **Build transparency:** Seeking help actively and communicating your expectations clearly builds openness and transparency, both of which are essential for practicing fairness. An innovative way to promote transparency is to clearly announce all the projects/initiatives where you need help and state your delivery expectations for each of the projects/initiatives. Let your team members apply, interview them as if you are considering a new member for the project. Based on the interview you allot the project. Communicate what criteria you used for selecting the person. This ensures that you are not seen as someone who indulges in favoritism.

5. **Reach out to encourage personal aspirations:** In each of your monthly/quarterly one to one reviews with each of your team members, spend the first 10 minutes discussing what they have done to build their resume in the last month/ quarter to realize their professional aspirations.

6. **Seek feedback about your leadership style:** When feedback becomes two-way it creates trust and promotes inter-dependence. Try asking your team to do a leadership audit every quarter and give you a scorecard on your leadership effectiveness. If you want your team to be accountable to you, you should also be accountable to your team members for providing the right leadership.

7. **Build positive energies:** In the morning of every working day, form an open circle and spend five minutes sharing the "Thought for the day." Hold hands in the circle and encourage your team to pass on positive energies to each other.

8. **Practice what you preach:** Values have to be lived on a daily basis. If practiced according to convenience, they are not values. Hence, if someone has attitude problems, treats women colleagues disrespectfully, breaches integrity – throw the person out immediately and tell your team

what happened. Your team should know that you are a soft manager with hard stances.

SKILLS TO BECOME A LEADER OF CHOICE

1. *Keeping your mouth shut and your mind open*: When members come to us with ideas we assume that we need to give our point of view. This affects our ability to listen as we are simultaneously processing and evaluating the idea. When we comment on the idea, at times we could be belittling or discounting their ideas. What if we take up our role of listening and mirror what the team member said as their idea? What if we take up the role of only seeking clarifications? For example if we were to say, This is what I understood. Did I get it right?" or "What do you mean when you say this? Can you help by becoming clearer?" rather than starting off with, "Well, I think….". Try it. When you mirror, you actually add significant value to the team member. You communicate to them that what they are saying matters and is significant. The team member feels respected and listened to.

2. *Tell stories that stick:* Map the significant highs and lows in your professional life. Convert each of the experiences into a teachable point of view. Use these stories to teach your team members valuable leadership lessons. Do it to help them and not to show off. If your intent is right you will come across as authentic.

3. *License to trip and learn:* Give a budget to team members to make 10 mistakes every month. However, members cannot repeat the mistake. When they make a mistake they have to share it with everyone to be able to use the mistake budget. Similarly, in review meetings, ask the people who have met and exceeded numbers to share what they have done well. Encourage each team member to ask as many questions to decipher the secret recipe of success. Then ask those who have not met numbers, what they can learn from these success stories and seek commitments. This way of review encourages group learning and growth.

4. *Use the 20% Principle:* 20% of work of each team member should consist of something they have never done before. It can be something that some other department does, or something their boss does or something that nobody has done. By encouraging people to do things they have never done, you encourage them to discover their hidden potential.

Developing skills to become a leader of choice requires deliberate practice. Actually this is the easier part. The more complex part is to develop the conviction that one does not want to remain a positional leader. It is so easy to draw power from the title, level and cabin space. It is easier to demand compliance. What is difficult is to earn the right to lead, stick to the path that generates trust and redefine the term leadership as an opportunity to kindle the magic in team members that mortals call as human talent.

LAP 2 – SECTOR III

TRUST-PERFORMANCE LEADERSHIP
– THE SOUL OF PIT STOP

In the following pages, there are a few cartoons to reflect different aspects of leadership. Have fun as you read them! And think about whether they mirror some of _your_ leadership behaviors.

What do you do when your team member is inundated with too much work?

How do you deal with a new member who has earlier worked for an organization with a different culture?

Is this how members from different departments in your organization work with each other?

When your boss gives his piece of mind to you, is there a cascading effect?

What do you say when your key employee expresses his desire to move into a new role in some other function?

Do you overwork a few employees?

Are people in your team under pressure to conform to others expectations or can they be themselves?

Which of these cartoons made you reflect on your current style of leading people? Is there anything that is blocking you from building Trust and becoming a Leader of Choice? Remember, unless you are a Leader of Choice your intentions will always be under the shadow of distrust. When people doubt your intentions, you cannot have great pit stops.

Tomorrow observe yourself in the office – in one to one interactions with your colleagues, in meetings, with internal customers, with your boss, in the canteen, in the field, wherever – what can you do consciously to become a Leader of Choice?

In the remaining part of the book, I would like to take you through a deeper understanding of pit stops at three levels - organizational, team and individual. While exploring pit stops at each of these levels, I would first like to present the notions that govern the way the pit stop is typically managed, and then using examples, provide the reader effective ways of structuring and facilitating these pit stops.

LAP 3

DOES YOUR ORGANIZATION VALUE PIT STOP REFLECTION?

LAP 3 – SECTOR I

DO YOUR ORGANIZATIONAL PIT STOPS HAVE THE ZING?

PLAN

ACT

DO

PITSTOP

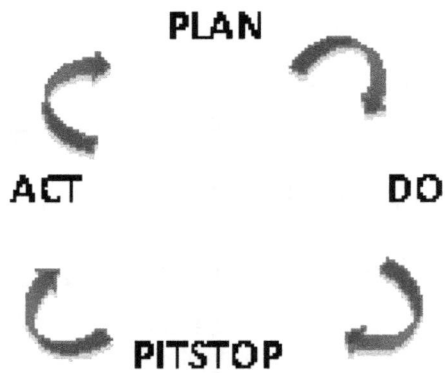

As an Organizational Leader do you value Reflection?

While reflecting, do you value who said it or what is said?

Let's be honest here. How do you conduct your yearly organizational reviews and planning meetings? If you were part of the majority, you would probably be doing it as a yearly ritual – a game that needs to be played. A game where there are no winners.

If ever you want to make a comedy show featuring organisations, the annual organizational review pit stop would be on top of the list. Given below are plot ideas which you can use. If any of these plots resonate with what happens in your organization, you are already living the comedy show – as a sidekick or better still the main character!!

PLOT 1: POWERPOINT ADVOCACY

Prepare PowerPoint presentations that conceal more than they reveal. Your goal is to convince your senior management that your department/business has done extremely well. You highlight your achievements and downplay what has not been achieved. You prepare well, anticipate questions, come up with well-rehearsed answers and aim for an appreciative nod or a clap from the audience.

The measure of success in such meetings is how you handled questions or objections, how well you argued that your approach is right and your achievements are par excellence. So you present information selectively, you interpret data as it suits you and use your convent English to great effect.

PLOT 2: THE ELDERS CLUB

If you are one of the designated wise old men of the company, this plot is tailor made for you. Isn't strategic thinking the prerogative of the senior management team? While many of us are politically right in saying no that is not so, and literate enough to read books on co-creation, when it comes to managing our own company we know intuitively that we, the elders of the company, know what is right for everyone. HODs and managers above deliberate on strategy and review the same. Elders like to do it in style. Hence, review retreats are reserved for Bangkok or Bali or the Bahamas. Elders have a sense that they know the customer, they know the environment and if something is not going right, the problem is with the customer or with the competitor or government or the like. In many ways these Elders have shaped the company's past successes and then become prisoners of what helped them to succeed in the past.

Interestingly most of the elders sitting in such reviews know their customers through market research surveys and employees through employee engagement surveys. They would probably have difficulty finding their way back if left somewhere in the factory. Most of them would never have sat in the workers canteen or talked to their young employees, though they may be discussing youth as their key customers for the future.

The best aspect of such retreats is that there is a pecking order even among the elders. Some are elderly elders and others are young elders. Elderly elders talk. When they talk, they declare decisions. Young elders make mild requests and then talk emphatically about the elderly elders' decisions and why they are dead right.

PLOT 3: CONFUSED HATS

People who generally attend planning and review meetings wear more than one hat – typically they wear a department head hat on a day-to-day basis and in the organizational planning and review meeting they are supposed to wear a business leader hat. As people are used to the department hat, they forget to take that off. So each one looks at business from their department lenses and not from multiple perspectives. Many times, review meetings are akin to the five blind men trying to make sense of an elephant. Everyone is totally right and everyone is totally wrong. As the CEO also comes from a functional background, the final decision is generally a sales decision or a finance decision or an operations decision based on the CEO's functional orientation. While everyone is supposed to be a leader, no one wears a business hat in the review meeting.

The review process itself is conducted in an interesting manner. Each functional head makes presentations. The CEO asks questions and reviews the function. Everyone waits for their turn and funnily no one speaks out of turn. After all, it is not their function. If they have a smart question, just as all lay people have, they would reserve it for informal gossip. Who wants to open their mouth and lose a peer? After all they need to work with each other beyond the meeting.

PLOT 4: "SACRED COWS" (ASSUMPTIONS AND PREMISES THAT ARE NEVER MEANT TO BE QUESTIONED)

The holy men holding the review meeting also carry several sacred cows for their comfort. After all this is how we have done business. This is what we did to be successful These are the industry rules. These are our competitors. These are our customers. We are not supposed to be doing in this manner and so on. So many sacred cows, so many constraints created that it is a wonder that you still hear the holiest man of the meeting shout aloud "I want innovation."

PLOT 5: CLARK KENT AND SUPERMAN

Commit less and achieve more. Be Clark Kent at the beginning of the year and surprise others by revealing yourself as Superman of your department. So review meetings become celebration events of how we pulled the rabbit out of our pockets. Nobody will discuss here how the supermen created havoc by putting pressure on the system, how the organisation lost people and in many cases customers and our reputation. While reviews happen annually for that year, the side effects of superman actions roll out over several years. Who cares about connecting the problems of today and the superman actions of yesteryears?

Are any of these situations familiar to you? Are your high potentials well ingrained in this review culture? If yes, only God can save your company and of course you. Maybe if you are serious about change, this book can help you.

Do you want to know what constitutes an effective organization level pit stop? Let us share a few examples with you.

Edward Jones: Strategic Plan Pit Stop

At Edward Jones, a Missouri-based investment firm, the Executive Committee invites all associates to participate in crafting the organization's Strategic Plan via a Five-year Plan website. Several thousand responses are received from employees across the company. Leaders take the input seriously, understanding that when employees are involved in firm-level initiatives, they have a greater buy-in to the firm and its future.

Have you ever felt that while leadership is responsible for strategic planning and review, they are not really best placed to make decisions? They are neither closest to customers nor the people who serve them. If you have had this feeling then you are bang on. Despite this, in the past the leadership team could still make smart decisions, as the external environment was relatively stable, industry categories were well defined (which means that you knew who your competitors were) and mistakes were not as costly as they are now. Everything is so dynamic now that leaders are better off not taking strategic decisions and interpreting strategic events unilaterally. Engaging employees across levels helps in connecting the dots and making sense of the changing environment, unfolding opportunities and looming threats.

While what Edward Jones does is commendable, they can further benefit by involving their customers, business partners in their strategic planning and review dialogues.

Leaders who craft organizational plans and conduct reviews without involving a wider cross section of the organization in dialogues (two way engaging conversations) are fooling themselves about strategy.

How to involve Employees in a Strategic Planning Pit Stop

The Vision Community exercise began in Zensar in 2001 when they were struggling for survival. The vision community was a great way to reach out to the young people in order to drive strategy.

What started as a desperate measure for survival is today an integral part of the strategic planning process at Zensar. This unique initiative managed to attract the attention of Harvard Business School (HBS) Professor David Garvin who converted it into a case study. Ask Garvin, the C. Roland Christensen Professor of Business Administration at HBS, what prompted him to write a case study on Zensar and he says it was the excellent execution of the vision community initiative. "The vision community is a rare case of an idea being great in theory and also remarkably effective in practice," says Garvin.

Dig deeper into the workings of vision communities and a pattern emerges; in every vision community, the core ideas are linked to a common theme each year. Over years, the topics have progressed from how to position and restructure the company, to how to function more efficiently, and what new business opportunities to tap.

Here's how it's done: after these ideas have been detailed, as was done at the kick-off in early September every year, the employees who are a part of the exercise select which ideas they'd like to work on. What follows next is the actual implementation process, which takes the better part of the year. While not all the ideas pan out as planned, the success rate has been heartening.

Do the ideas generated in Vision Community translate into revenues or does it remain a motivational and bonding exercise that many initiatives of this sort degenerate into? According to Natarajan, almost Rs 400 crore out of the Rs 600 crores of new revenue has come through initiatives undertaken through a vision community idea. "Remote infrastructure management, one of our fastest growing businesses, was a vision community idea," says Natarajan. Today, the business contributes 9% to Zensar's total revenue.

Source: Economic Times

Engaging young minds for ideas is a great way of conducting the strategic planning and review pit stop. The Vision Community pit stop of Zensar also serves as an opportunity to develop business leadership. Great organizational pit stop. However, there are two flaws. Maybe flaw is a strong word. There are two opportunities to realize the full potential of the Vision Community pit stop. Every year the leadership team defines the broad themes. These themes direct the flow of employee ideas. What if the theme is wrong? Or there is a better theme? Or there is a need to look at several themes together? Engaging employees to identify the right themes may actually help in getting a sharper strategic focus. Also how can one say that the 80 odd people who are selected for this exercise are the right people? Why should an organization not look at the entire employee force for ideas? Given that the company is into IT, it may not be difficult for them to engage without disrupting work.

Leveraging IT for engaging the entire work force in a Culture Shaping Pit Stop

Since 2001, IBM has used jams to involve its more than 300,000 employees around the world in far-reaching exploration and problem solving.

In 2003, IBM undertook the first reexamination of its values in nearly 100 years. Through "Values-Jam," an unprecedented 72-hour discussion on IBM's global intranet, 319,000 IBMers around the world were invited to engage in an open "values jam" on their global intranet.

IBMers by the tens of thousands came together to define the essence of the company. They were thoughtful and passionate about the company they wanted to be a part of. They were also brutally honest. Some of what they wrote was painful to read, because they pointed out all the bureaucratic and dysfunctional things that get in the way of serving clients, working as a team or implementing new ideas. But the leadership team was resolute in keeping the dialog free flowing and candid. This resulted in a broad, enthusiastic, grass-roots consensus, which could not have been obtained in any other way.

In the end, IBMers determined that their actions would be driven by these values:

1. Dedication to every client's success

2. Innovation that matters, for our company and for the world

3. Trust and personal responsibility in all relationships.

I am sharing the World Jam process again. However this is in the context of architecting the culture of the organization. In many companies leaders define culture and expect people to align. This is a simplistic way of leading people. Unless people reflect, unless they appreciate why they should change and how that is going to benefit them – why should you expect that change would happen?

Leaders need to invest in an organizational pit stop to galvanize change. This is what Aviva did for an organizational pit stop to co-create a vision.

Organizational Pit Stop for Co-creating Vision

Aviva organized a visioning exercise called 'Navkriti — the spirit of life,' an energizing process that involved people in establishing the core values of the organization, and to be party to creating a compelling vision statement for the Company.

Over 150 employees across the country participated in this exercise through a series of workshops and forums, with the rest being involved through a series of questionnaires. As a conclusion to this activity, a series of communication exercises were conducted which included:

1. 800 individually addressed letters, each personally signed by the MD.

2. Thematic desk calendars around the values and key behavior indicators

3. Dynamic screen savers for all PCs/laptops capturing company values and the vision statement as well as moments of the workshops,

4. Inclusion of a special module on Navkriti in Induction Programs for new employees.

5. A special section in the online HR room on the process of the workshop, Aviva's vision, values and expected behaviors.

Better still, Eureka Forbes created an extended culture champions forum and planned pit stops for reviewing, envisioning, planning and implementing the desired culture.

> **Eureka Forbes:** has created a system similar to the parliamentary system, so that problems and issues, big and small, can be communicated effectively from their zonal and regional offices to headquarters. 270 candidates contest for 56 seats (42 Councilors and 14 Senators). Those elected are mandated to be emissaries of the head office in zonal offices. They draft their own manifestos and articulate plans to develop their constituencies. A senator, Mr. Ganesh, has taken up a lot of issues with the head office. He has helped structure salaries, incentives and rewards for his local team, after asking them how they would like to be paid. The biggest initiative was the Dream Bike scheme. In 2009, he received a lot of complaints from salespersons – called Euro Champs – saying they needed to upgrade the motorcycle the company had given them for work. The amount designated by the company for purchasing motorcycles had not been revised in several years. Ganesh sat with his team and worked out a barter arrangement. Each Euro champ agreed to make one extra sale for an enhanced motorcycle allowance. Faced with a revenue jump of almost 4 crores due to the extra sales, the head office agreed to hike up the allowance to Rs. 80,000. Ganesh says he could not have done all this but for the fact that he was member of the senate.
>
> (taken from http://articles.economictimes.indiatimes. com/2010-11-12/news/27609177_1_eureka-forbes-efl-representatives).

What if you are not managing your organizational pit stops in the manner described above. You are conducting pit stops in the conventional way and are still making money. Do you really need to change? Why can't you continue doing the same? What makes it imperative that you change your way of conducting organizational pit stops?

I. Failures have become costly

The average longevity of senior managers in an organization is less than 3 years. And, for lateral hires it is even lesser. Investors, Boards and Entrepreneurs are less forgiving of professional managers than they were before. The reason is because any strategic mistake takes the company backward, and in many cases puts the company out of reckoning.

II. The external environment has become complex and how

The days of simplistic interpretation of customer segmentation and competitor understanding are over. A deadly cocktail of factors are changing the aspiration and expectation of customers. These include changes in the political scenario, technology explosion in the form of internet and cell-phone communication options, economy, television, higher risk taking behavior among first time entrepreneurs and changing power equations in the Indian family. Sitting at the top of the hierarchy, senior leaders neither know customers intimately nor do they have the time and aptitude to deeply connect with front line employees. Scenario thinking would definitely help. This refers to thinking of "what if" possibilities – both realistic and outrageous – and preparing accordingly. Scenario thinking helps one prepare for eventualities of all kinds and converting threats into opportunities. Can you think of a better way of remaining agile and improving your response time? I doubt it. However, if you are three dimensional, how can you understand a multi dimensional universe?

III. Customer profiles are fast changing and the top management in many companies are far removed from this reality

In the past, upper and middle class constituted the bulk of the customer base. Branding and value propositions were largely targeted at this customer population. In the past, the top management in many companies, who hailed from premier engineering and management colleges, could easily connect with and understand these customers. Now the customer base is changing. Does the top management of an MNC really understand the mindset of the neo rich of Gurgaon – the shepherd who owns a Mercedes thanks to the real estate boom? Or does it understand the lower middle class which lives in a slum but spends thousands on their lifestyle or children's coaching classes? No wonder then that the top management of many MNC's in India are not able to dislodge the stronghold of the informal sector. They do not engage enough. In many companies brand managers strategise for rural clients without having spent a single day in a village or even making an attempt to understand the aspirations of rural India. Why is it that Nestle can never hope to have the presence Amul has in rural Indian markets? Because decision making in Amul happens by people who closely engage with and know the rural market. Similarly, Ghari detergent has taken rural markets by storm and is leaving its competitors such as Nirma and Wheel, way behind. The advertisements selling Ghari detergent, have a strong rural ambience, they desist from using celebrities to endorse their product and they keep costs down by spending very less on marketing or hiring MBA's from premier institutes. When a company hires people who are from a similar background as the customers they seek to service they are able to empathise much better with the needs of the clients and sharply target their products and services to delight their target audience.

IV. The front line is smarter

The profile of the front line sales executive, the front line workmen and the supervisor is changing drastically. The sales person is no longer a compliant doer. She is also a thinker. She is confident and has aspirations. Similarly, the factory work is no longer a function of physical prowess. It is about working smart using logic control systems. When the collective IQ of the organization is higher than before, using outdated organizational structures and systems is a real pity. We can do much more and get much more with the quality of talent that is there at the grass root level in every organization.

These developments require organizations to re-examine the way they conduct their organizational planning and review pit stops. The days of strategic planning and review as a preserve of an elite group are over. Such pit stops serve no purpose. The time has come to engage diverse stakeholders in organizational pit stops - bring in stakeholders of different kinds and co-create the company's future. This sounds laudable but is it practical? How can we plan, manage and execute such it stops to get maximum value? How can we get the most out of organizational pit stops involving the larger organization and diverse stakeholder groups? The next section explores some of these questions.

Lap 3 – Sector II

Ideas to Strengthen your Organizational Pit Stops

At the outset I present below ideas about what has to change in the way organizational pit stops are normally conducted.

Idea 1: Use the organizational pit stop as an opportunity to know the best of what we have done during the last year and dig deeper into what enabled our success

"Ok, we did a great job last year. Lets all pat ourselves. However, we need to move on and set new goals. Let's examine the mistakes and missed opportunities and what we can learn from them."

Is this how your senior leaders speak? If they do speak this way, this is the first thing that they should change about the way they conduct this pit stop.

Ignoring what we did or did not do last year is not leveraging our learning from the last year. Similarly, focusing only on what we did not do right is underestimating our collective potential. If only we look into what we did right, we can understand how certain people, certain teams and parts of the organization are responding well to the changing needs of the external environment. This helps those who are currently not aligned with the external environment to learn how to do the same. The pit stop then becomes an accelerated learning for the entire organization.

Idea 2: Engage everyone in organization level planning and reviews

Every individual in the organization brings in a worldview that is unique and contributes to an understanding of the whole picture. Losing one worldview is like losing a piece of the puzzle – the puzzle will never be complete. A question that you may have is "Isn't it unrealistic to involve every employee in the organizational planning and review?"

- **Use technology**: Internet, intranet, video conferencing, tele-conferencing are options that enable you to connect with your entire population. Use it effectively.

- **Use emails:** Start a group email that engages people on key questions. Use one question at a time and get responses. Give prizes for insights, participation and contrarian views. The questions could be:

  1. What is the best that we as an organization, department, and team accomplished that we feel proud of? What did we do which contributed to the success? What did we learn from each of the successes?

  2. What is it that we do right now that we should continue doing? What is the one thing that we should change?

  3. In the last one year – What is the one big change that you see in the market? What's the one big change you see about our customers? What is the one big change you see about our competitors?

  4. If you are the CEO, one new idea that you will pursue which you believe has great potential?

  5. What about our culture is helping us and what about our culture is hindering us from achieving our strategy?

- **Use the large-scale interactive process (LSIP) methodology as a way to engage with a large number of stakeholders simultaneously**: LSIP is a powerful methodology wherein you can involve hundreds of people simultaneously and conduct an interactive dialogue. Apart from employees, you can involve customers, suppliers, and industry experts in this process. Listening to stakeholder voices helps in understanding the impact that you have created during the last twelve months, how the external environment is shaping up and how the expectations of the stakeholders are changing accordingly.

Here's a story of how the magic of LSIP can be used to conduct an organizational pit stop. This case let is based on a real consulting work designed and facilitated by me. I changed the name of the client company for confidentiality purposes.

Large Scale Change Management in a PE led Bio Technology and Pharmaceutical Company

Background

Ranova Limited is a diversified pharmaceutical company that provides laboratory solutions, conducts chemical research and develops medicines for veterinary care. Ranova used to be part of a large Indian pharmaceutical company. The Indian pharmaceutical company sold Ranova to a Private Equity (PE) firm. The PE firm gave stock option to the ten member top management team, gave them strategic and operational freedom and retained them. Together the top team owns 5% of the total stake.

Context for change

The PE ownership of Ranova Limited created an air of uncertainty among its 400 employees about their future in the company. From the time its ownership changed, one could not help but notice several unproductive and dysfunctional conversations at Ranova. Work started getting affected. The senior management team wanted employees to understand that while no PE firm would hold on to their investment for ever, they would also not want to let go of valuable employees. The key to success was to stay focused on continuous learning, to be positively restless, set challenging goals and deliver excellence consistently. There were town hall meetings, memos, and departmental meetings to help people settle down. However this did not have the necessary effect. At this point, Ranova engaged a consulting firm to support them in allaying the fears of employees and bringing in a more positive, forward-looking work culture.

The consulting firm recommended that if employees could seek inspiration from things that will never change, they would find it easy to navigate the uncertainties of PE ownership. These unchanging things included Vision, Values and Winning Habits. However these could not be downloaded on employees. Inspiration comes from within; hence it had to be discovered.

To facilitate this, the consulting firm recommended a large-scale interactive process (LSIP) methodology. They recommended holding an organizational pit stop for the entire workforce of approximately 550 people.

However, the consulting firm felt it was important to prepare the senior management team of the organization on their leadership role during and after the organizational pit stop. This was necessary because often, during such pit stops leaders get into a 'telling' mode instead of engaging in self-reflection. Similarly after an LSIP based organizational pit stop, the organizational culture and attitudes of employees change dramatically. Therefore, a leadership style that is not aligned to an empowering culture but is based on command and control, does not work in the post LSIP environment. The consulting firm helped the senior management team to reflect on their leadership style and the kind of style that will nurture and grow the post LSIP environment organizational culture.

Designing the pit stop

In a large-scale interactive (LSIP) process external experts and event management companies do not run the event. Internal teams create the intervention design (including the LSIP event design) and also manage its logistics and the overall program. This is because employees best understand what are the pain areas, what they want to create and what will work. In other words they are the content experts for their organization. In such a context, the consultant is a process facilitator. He/she provides questions as thinking tools and creates a process wherein participants can arrive at the most appropriate agenda, objectives, methodology and logistics management. Therefore, the first step towards conducting the pit stop consisted of creating a design and a logistics team. The design team consisted of a representative sample of employees across all levels and functions. Similarly a logistics team was constituted, with a heavier presence of veterans from the administration department, although some representatives from other functions were also included.

The LSIP pit stop

As participants entered the LSIP event room, they were in for a surprise. There were round tables in the room as opposed to theatre style seating, which was the norm. Seven participants sat on each table. Between them they represented the diversity of the organization – different departments and different levels. Unlike conventional pit stops where there is a down load of information and perspectives from seniors, the LSIP pit stop began with participants at each table sharing their hopes, fears and ideas for making the organization and themselves successful. This process was called 'Telling our Stories'. After participants shared their stories, the consolidated output was documented on flip charts and displayed for every one to walk around and absorb. As participants went through each others' charts, they began to realize there was so much in common among them. These shared thoughts and feelings brought people together. From perceiving each other as disparate, they began to experience a sense of being part of a community with shared dreams, concerns and ideas to make the company a better place to work and perform. At this stage the facilitators introduced a change framework for becoming a great place to work and perform. This framework stated that change happens when people are dissatisfied with the present, have a shared vision for the future and experiment new behaviors to change the present and create the future. To create dissatisfaction with the present, Ranova's customers, suppliers, industry experts were invited to share what the organization and people needed to change to be able to meet their expectations in the present and future. Each conversation with the stakeholders was interactive and engaging. Leaders from the PE firm were asked to speak on how they assessed high performance and what was their advice for Ranova with respect to building a high performance culture. After listening and absorbing the feedback given by various stakeholders, the employees wanted to get into action planning. After all there was so much food for thought. But the facilitators discouraged the participants to get into action planning at this stage, based on what others had said- even if these others constituted their important stakeholders. Their logic was that actions could not be sustained if they were driven only by external feedback. The impetus for sustainable growth had to come from an inspiring shared dream. Using an interesting participatory methodology the facilitators helped the group to articulate the kind of organization they wanted to become. Once the vision was in place, action planning followed. Most of the time action steps created at the end of an organizational pit stop do not work because of pressing demands of day-to-day work. Hence in LSIP, action planning involves sharing expectations between departments, between hierarchical levels on what needs to change with respect to work behaviors, structure, systems, processes and skills in order to change the present and create the desired future. At the end of the organizational pit stop, one could experience the determination to make it happen among all the employees of Ranova. There was no skepticism as all those who needed to influence and be influenced were there in the LSIP pit stop. Every one had common data, a common understanding, a common vision and shared actions.

The LSIP process had been like a total healing experience–healing of the body, mind and the spirit. Change was visible from the next day on-wards and the organization set forth on a sustainable growth path.

Epilogue

Ranova continues the practice of LSIPs for addressing other organizational challenges. Mini-LSIPs are now common in Ranova. They consciously desist from making grand plans in a cabin and then ruing about why people do not want to follow management policies. LSIP engages with the organization as a whole rather than adopting a piece meal approach to problem solving. One year after the large-scale change process, Ranova Limited has been ranked amongst the top 50 companies to work for in India and No.1 in the Biotechnology and Pharmaceuticals segment. In 2011 Ranova was sold to a global pharma major. The management reports that this has not lead to any dip in high performance or engagement of employees.

Idea 3: Conduct the pit stop as a bottom up dialogue

Generally goal setting and review exercises in organizations are top down processes. Goals are set at the top and they cascade downwards. If you examine the KRA's of the senior leadership in your organization, you will find that they are accountable for reducing costs, increasing revenues, profitability and securing growth. These goals are broken down further and distributed across employees. So a revenue goal of the CEO or the Sales Head would have been distributed between the sales executives of your organization. Now through the year a significant part of what the CEO or the Sales Head does is to review the goal, bring in a sense of urgency and ensure everyone is focused on chasing the goal. However, the bottom line is that this is hardly why we hire and pay hefty salaries to senior leaders. In reality, the problem originates from the way this pit stop is conducted. It is done as a top down process. What if you turn the conventional wisdom upside down and conduct this goal setting pit stop as a bottom up process?

The section below describes how this can be done.

1ˢᵗ Step Look at the diagram on the following page. What does it tell you? Front line employees in your organization can and should provide the basic raw material for goal setting. Front line employees include supervisors and front line managers as well as those who are engaged in directly producing and/or selling products and services to your customers. In knowledge management companies' front line employees would include project managers and those below. There is a sound logic as to why front liners should be engaged first in goal setting. Since this is the group that has to deliver the tangible goals of the organization, it is common sense that they should be setting the goals. But what they may not have is the worldview and perspective to undertake goal setting. This is where middle and senior managers have to play a significant facilitative role by bringing in customer voices, market research data, advice from industry experts and marketing specialists to deepen the understanding of front line staff. By creating the right conditions, one finds very often that front liners are able to visualize opportunities and set goals that are far more challenging and ambitious than senior management. Therefore, engage your front line sales, operations and support staff in a review and planning dialogue. Let them share their goals for the organization, current market trends, ideas and goals for the next year. That is let them get involved in developing strategic plans that flow from their own aspirations as well as the market potential to achieve this aspiration.

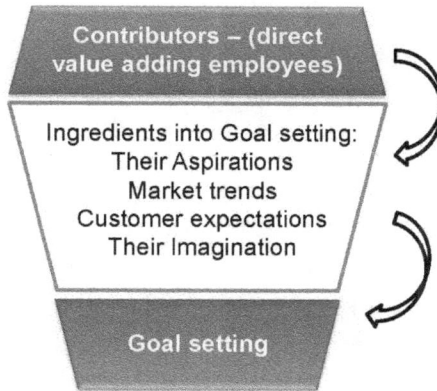

After setting their goals, the team should also identify the support required from their managers to enable them to achieve these goals. These include system/process improvements, infrastructure, capability, up-gradation and coaching support.

2ⁿᵈ Step Now move a level above- your middle management. Engage your middle level managers to dialogue on how they can enable the front line to achieve their goals. In this dialogue, they use the feedback of the front line. This apart, they would also discuss how to ensure that departments work in a seamless manner, how to ensure that employees in the organization know how customers are experiencing the company's services and how to build capabilities in the frontline to act as leaders and not just as followers.

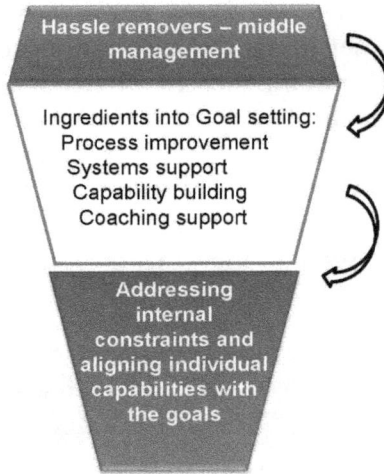

3rd ***Step*** Senior Management absorbs the output from the frontline and middle management and dialogues on how to enhance the capacity of the organization to deliver effortlessly. This includes developing a learning culture, making/revising relevant policies and systems, eliminating outdated policies/ systems, designing and driving leadership development, succession planning, technology up-gradation and coaching managers.

The goals that front line staff set would be measurable sales/service/product goals. The goals that middle management sets would improve processes and build internal capabilities. The goals set by senior leadership would enable middle management to be effective and prepare the organization for the future. Now the pit stops are not places where people play dirty games but places where we set game changing agendas.

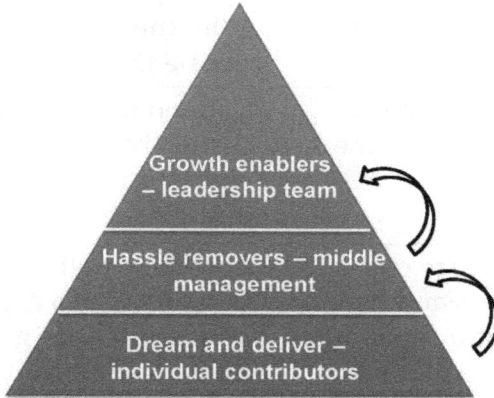

In the bottom up goal setting process, the leadership team sets growth enabling goals, the middle management sets goals that address constraints and the individual contributors at the front lines set delivery focused goals. Now we have a pit stop that positions the organization for success.

Idea 4: Make your Organizational pit stop into a collective learning and unlearning exercise.

Listen to any speech that a CEO makes or a presentation in an organization meeting and you can document at least half a dozen sacred cows (assumptions) that the organization has taken for granted and is making plans around.

I was once engaged by an automotive component company, which worked through Joint Ventures. The foreign partner would bring technical inputs and the Indian counterpart would manage operations. An assumption that dictated the Indian company's actions was that the foreign partner did not know about the way employee relations are managed in India and hence would be happy to restrict themselves to providing only technical leadership. This was their sacred cow. They did not realize that the foreign partner was examining the quality of their management, critically. Over a period of time they lost faith and patience in the Indian company's ability to deliver and decided to part ways.

Which sacred cows afflict you?	Why the sacred cows may not be that holy
We are indispensible partners to our customers	Sudden market changes, disruptive technologies and simply a need to manage risk and cost
Our suppliers are our junior partners and their aspirations and capabilities are limited.	People as well as Organization's aspirations and capabilities grow over time. At some point a supplier may want to leverage on their experience, enter your space and make more money. Remember HTC and INTEX?
Our competitors are part of our industry and are very much like us (size, thinking, executing and way of working).	If this sacred cow is right Moser Baer should not have entered the video CD market, Apple should not have anything to do with music as it is a computer company.

Anybody who does not think like us is stupid and doomed to fail	Celebrated management teams who thought that Amazon does not stand a chance of selling books online. Aggressive leaders who bulldozed their sales and marketing teams into believing that it is impossible to sell shampoo to a village girl? What she wants is just a soap like Lifebuoy.
Our industry is distinct. We need our kind of experience when we hire people.	What if the HR heads of automotive companies experiencing high attrition thought of a gentlemen's contract not to hire people from each other's companies? They could get into trouble if IT companies start the trend of hiring people from the automotive sector as project managers. They may find such people's skills in project and team management valuable. Can an industry stop the flow of talent to other sectors with this gentlemen's contract?

If the organizational planning and review pit stop focuses on identifying and challenging sacred cows, it becomes a valuable reflection process. Otherwise it is a sham exercise that pushes the organization towards greater danger.

As your understanding of organizational pit stop changes, it also changes your perspective about your own role as a leader. You are not here to provide direction. You are here to create a robust process that helps in discovering the direction. As people have a say in the reviewing and strategizing of pit stops, they also become committed to implementing decisions. They understand what is important and what is urgent and prioritize their work and collaborate with each other on their own.

By leveraging the trust that you built through respect, fairness and authenticity you can convert your organizational pit stops into a performance engine.

LAP 3 – SECTOR III

DO YOU HAVE ORGANIZATIONAL PIT STOPS TO SPOT THE SPARK BEFORE IT BECOMES A RAGING FIRE?

In Eicher, an operator could stop the machine and call for a pit stop discussion on poor quality.

Can your frontline employees do the same when they sense a crisis – within the organization or at the marketplace?

Let's say there is some development in the market that could cause a threat to your organization. Your frontline sales staff has sensed this, though they may not be able to confidently explain the enormity of the situation. Can any of them call for a pit stop with your senior management to discuss the development? Are they empowered to do this? Do they feel empowered?

If there is a huge time lag between someone in the organization noticing a development (an opportunity or a threat) and your leadership team actually holding a pit stop to discuss the same – the company is not smart in its unplanned pit stops.

Whenever there are any changes in customer preferences or market trends, the person to first know about it is the individual who is closest to your customer – could be your frontline salesman or even better the sales person of your dealer. They can sniff changes, just like birds and animals do when there is an impending earthquake or a tsunami – and they can sniff all this fairly early. The information they have is seldom straightforward. It is bits of messy information; an intuitive feeling that something is not all right or something is changing fundamentally. Is there a way in which this information can reach the higher ups? Can they call for a meeting, citing an emergency? This is very unlikely. Until a market research agency gives a heads up or the crisis has precipitated enough to become self evident to everyone – leaders do not act upon and call for a pit stop meeting. Even when such a meeting is called, those invited do not include the frontline people. It will include all those whose backs are on fire and hence have a need to under-emphasize the gravity of the situation. Finally, the entire team would live in denial until someone from the top asks the leadership team to shape up or step out.

What is your own sense about the crisis at Kingfisher or Sahara? Did no one in the organization know of the impending disaster? You do not need to be a consultant from McKinseys to put two and two together and conclude that it is just a matter of time.

Read the story below. It is incredible.

In early 2012, Sony introduced Tablet P, the company's attempt to make tablets an even more portable experience. The P features a unique clamshell design, allowing the device to fold in half and fit into a pocket. This feature, however, also resulted in a flaw that ruined the device for most users. In order to make it foldable, the screen is split in half by a large, black hinge, which makes playing games and reading incredibly awkward. Because of the screen split, as well as complaints about the operating system and touchscreen sensitivity, the P garnered horrible reviews. In response to poor sales, the device was sold at a steep discount — dropping from $549 to $199 — within a few months. In August, Sony announced it would be updating the Android operating system to the latest "Jellybean" version for the Sony Tablet S, but that the P would not be updated. The company is no longer selling the tablet on its American website.

Is it possible at all that when the product was being discussed at the development stage, no one in Sony had an issue with the fold and its impact on the quality of viewing? It seems pretty obvious that a split screen would make viewing awkward. Maybe a few strong personalities in the company were wedded to the design and nobody dared to call for a meeting and ask questions.

For that matter, look at this.

POND'S TOOTHPASTE

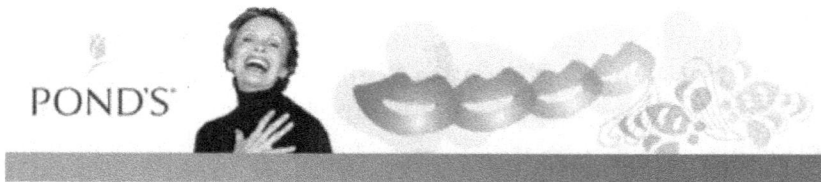

Isn't the thought nauseating? Pond's is known for skin cream, something you apply on your skin. Introducing toothpaste with the same name? It's like Harpic introducing beauty products. Sounds yucky, isn't it?

The point is not to discuss why the product failed in the market. The point is, was there an organizational culture and mechanism for someone in Pond's to call for an impromptu pit stop to discuss their concern that this was not going to work? Having interacted with market researchers extensively, I can say with confidence that even market researchers are scared to tell the king that he is naked. No one would have called for an unplanned pit stop to discuss the concern or the market research data and relook at the product name or even the product introduction under the brand name. After spending several crores to make the product work, the company took it off the shelves.

TAKE A LOOK AT THIS PRODUCT

How did CK Ranganathan take on the Goliaths of Indian FMCG and survive? How did CavinKare's Chik shampoo grow right under the noses of Hindustan Levers and P&G and continue to become a thorn in their side? After Chik's success, former Hindustan Levers executive director Dalip Sehgal, who worked for the FMCG giant between 1982 and 2007, acknowledged that Ranganathan possessed strong insights into the mind of the consumer.

Can you believe that nobody from the sales field staff of Unilever India and P&G India had enough insight from the initial success of Chik shampoo to understand that the rural market was aspirational and was willing to pay more for small quantity premium products? I bet there were many who felt the success of Chik was a breakthrough. However, there was no way they could influence and change the thinking of the senior leadership of their companies. There was no unplanned pit stop that they could call for. If only they could, they could have not only killed Chik shampoo but also taken advantage of the new found love of the rural customer.

Does your organization have a culture where people across levels can call for an unplanned pit stop with the senior management? Apart from the hierarchy issue, people feel uncomfortable discussing such issues as no one really knows what will actually work. While success makes a decision wise, failure automatically labels the person with a valid concern as a wet blanket. To overcome this Federal Express has legitimized unplanned pit stops. They have an institution called the Supreme Court of FedEx wherein even the CEO's decisions can be challenged. This institution creates an opportunity for an unplanned pit stop. Smart, isn't it?

If you are a sports lover, you would appreciate the value of the two appeals that each team has which needs to be adjudicated by the third umpire. This creates an opportunity for a re-look and some times overturning a decision that the umpire has taken.

How to institutionalize Effective Unplanned Pit Stops

It is not wise to assume that by using a conventional organization structure, formal forums and communication systems, it is possible to spot opportunities or to become aware of threats. Structure, forums and systems ensure predictability. They promote stability not chaos. Imagine you come to work with a clear plan about how you want to spend the day. You are clear about what you want to achieve at the end of the day. You have detailed out your time schedule and come to the office determined that you will make your plan work.

Let's say as soon as you come into the office there is some unexpected visitor or an unexpected development. Your intent would be to quickly address the emergency and revert to your original plan. This is how organizations become effective in operations. Plan and do as per the plan. Companies celebrate predictability. What if some unsettling opportunity or threat comes to their notice? Typically, a 'smart' person would quickly underplay the opportunity as a passing fad or something that is not aligned to the current strategy. Similarly, people also tend to blame the threat perception to over-imagination of the messenger and worse still, label the messenger as someone who is incapable of handling issues on his own. When aberrations occur contrary to the set course it is important to take cognizance, reflect and adapt to the new situation.

In this context, I wish to share with you examples of companies, which have created and promoted un-planned pit stops effectively.

BEER BARS TO BOUNCE BACK

When the new Heineken CEO took office, the company was in the middle of a tough financial situation. The morale of employees was low and attrition was high. Employees expected the new CEO to take tough cost cutting measures. Instead, the CEO did something weird. There were several empty spaces in the Heineken building as several employees had left. He converted a large empty space into a beer bar. Beer was served free. Doesn't it sound stupid? Spending money on free beer for employees when the company is doing badly? What the beer bar did was to bring people of different departments together. Sitting in the beer bar, they not only had fun but also discussed business. Several unplanned pit stops happened spontaneously everyday, and it led to optimal decisions in contrast to sub optimal department oriented decisions. Very soon the company turned around.

Boundary Spanners at Southwest – facilitators of unplanned pit stops

Boundary spanners are people who bring together information from different operating units of the business. They help to build relationships between different parts of the organization around common goals and mutual respect, so the organization can operate more cohesively. They help departments to surface and address the differences with other departments.

Most companies use information technology as a platform for sharing information between one business unit to another. Southwest took the opposite approach. It has strengthened the role of on-site operations agents who are responsible for turning around each Southwest flight as rapidly as possible. As boundary spanners, the on-site operations agent takes a more holistic perspective – whereas people closely involved in running one or another function rarely have the time to stop and consider the bigger picture. Boundary spanners share that broader viewpoint to help others work more effectively. In doing so they create effective unplanned pit stops.

How do they manage to do that?

They build relationships across boundaries – meaning there will be a broader sense of shared identity and shared vision between parties whose interests may not always mesh together. As a result, collective actions become more effective. The boundary spanners play a key social role – since they represent the point at which the efforts of one unit or department mesh with those of other units or departments. By having a real life person in this role rather than a computer, there is the opportunity for relationships to grow and be strengthened. In effect, the boundary spanner puts a human face on the combined work of both teams.

Go Meet Anyone

Intel practices a strong sense of egalitarianism and openness. Any employee can set up one-on-one meetings with anyone, no matter how senior they are, and go talk to them. No one has walled offices. Wow! This is a great, unplanned pit stop opportunity.

COMPANY GOSSIP BLOG

Steven Johnson talks about 'Slow Hunches' in his book *Where Good Ideas Come from*. If you have not already read it, you must-it's a great book for leaders to read. People have gut feelings, unsubstantiated ideas, and bits of small information about the market, competitors, customers, trends etc. In isolation they do not make sense and are also of little value. However, it is possible to gain insights and make sense of these seemingly unconnected facts by connecting the dots. How about a company gossip blog that is playful and lots of fun? It would legitimize sharing concerns, issues, and ideas across levels, locations, and departments. It would reduce the time gap between the early crisis signal and the actual pit stop.

PLANNING FOR THE UNINTENDED CONSEQUENCES

Why should an unplanned pit stop be called for only when there is a real opportunity or threat? What if we are able to visualize the same and be prepared to handle the same? When organizations make goals, they are basically working towards certain intended outcomes. However, there are several unintended side effects that each goal may lead to. These could be positive or negative. Positive side effects constitute opportunities and those, which are negative, are potential threats. Let's say, you have set an organizational goal to enter a virgin market and sell premium shoes. You have inadvertently created an aspirational demand for neckties. This is an opportunity. However, at the same time, there may be issues related to the use of animal skin in the communities you service. This could provoke protests and create bad publicity. This is the unintended consequence of the goal. Creating spaces to visualize and articulate the unintended consequences, good and bad, builds trust and strengthens unplanned pit stops as a process.

CELEBRATING THE CULTURE OF COURAGE

You should feel proud of yourself if someone whose role it is not to do so, makes a big noise and brings an issue to the attention of the management. You have created an environment where people are courageous to ask for time outs and passionate about making the organization successful. Effective unplanned pit stops are a result of your leadership. Congratulations. When you demonstrate respect a call for an unplanned pit stop by focusing on the intent rather than who is raising the issue; when you listen with an open mind; when you encourage honest conversations you have made each unplanned pit stop valuable and also future, effective, unplanned, pit stops possible.

You would have realized the power of organizational pit stops. I hope you will review your planned and unplanned organizational pit stops critically and enhance their effectiveness.

Now let's move on.

In the next section we shall explore the value of effective team pit stops.

LAP 4
TEAM PIT STOPS

Lap 4 – Sector I
Are your Team Pit Stops dung pits?

If we can get time off from meetings, we can do our real work

Do you have too many meetings in your organization? When you come to work in the morning, have you already started planning to do 'real work' from 5 p.m. onwards? If you are really smart, you would have found a way to deal with umpteen meetings, one after another – enter the meeting, open up your laptop and smartphone and continue your real work while pretending to listen to what is happening in the meeting. You might have found that this is actually a great way to accomplish a lot of work without getting disturbed.

If this resonates with your experience, let's admit the truth. Team pit stops are not working in your organization, they have become a bloody waste of time. Most bad team pit stops take the following forms.

Delhi Darbars

You may have experienced leaders who like to have their own darbars. They like the feel of many people around them to conduct daily matters. Several cups of coffee and several plates of 'Good Day' biscuits appear and disappear. The meetings generally start at 11 a.m. and end by 2 p.m., just in time for a long lunch. After that there is just enough time for each of the participants to go back to their teams and have their own small darbars. Meetings become the reason for work, or better still meetings are work. The discussions waver and seldom are minutes of meetings documented and people are not made accountable in the subsequent meetings.

Sleight of Numbers

These meetings are all about numbers. Presenters juggle between power point and excel documents. These meetings resemble weather updates. Sales are down by 5%; operations are up by 20%; waste is 4.3% of revenues and so on and on. There are plenty of pie charts, bar graphs, smart power point entries and exits through custom animation. Also a few questions here and there and lots of yawns. There are smart-ass presenters and several asses who bring their team members to make their presentations. Most presentations are the read only kind – no discussion, no deeper analysis.

CHAKRAVYUH

More than 2000 years back in the war that took place at Kurukshetra, the Kauravas found that the best way to deal with the young Abhimanyu was by fighting against him in a group. Many team leaders seek inspiration from this story. They conduct individual reviews in team meetings. The leader takes pleasure in pinning the team member down. The submissive team member will readily cave in. The aggressive team member will try to argue. However, in a large group he knows his status as a loner. Generally peers do not come to the rescue. After all, their role is that of gladiators watching the fight and once their peer is finished, they are next in line. It is better to neither support nor oppose. After all it is not their department. Be a spectator and wait for your turn.

Do any of these resonate with you? Why do you think bad team pit stops happen? Is there a way out? Can we really make planned team pit stops effective? Team pit stops are useful only if they contribute any of the following in an effective manner.

COLLECTIVE LEARNING

This is not about knowing each other's functions better. Collective learning is about connecting the dots and understanding how to make the team successful. It is about developing a systems understanding. If we take the analogy of the body – if different body parts come for a team meeting, collective learning is not so much about each part knowing about the other parts. It is about understanding the role one's own part plays in making the other parts successful. It is about gaining an insight into how to collaborate and achieve synergies.

PROBLEM SOLVING

Teams value speed. They value quick problem solving. However, in the process they often mistake symptoms for problems. For instance, if there is a problem with teamwork, many teams respond by saying let's go for an outing together or let's have a team-building workshop. This is a quick fix approach to problems. You fixed it. It never got resolved. And that is why it is likely to recur. If teamwork is the issue, the first question to ask is how do we define teamwork? The second question should be, is teamwork really required? If the answer to question two is yes, we need to then brainstorm on why teamwork is not happening. The actual problem could be lack of physical proximity or lack of common performance metrics or lack of feedback or something else. It may not be a trust issue. Or maybe it is. Coming up with quick solutions to problems may be heroic but may lead the team on an entirely wrong path. \

DECISION-MAKING

At the core, we are all paid to take decisions and make them work through effective implementation. If decisions are taken based on what worked in the past or if they are based on the least risk theory – the team pit stop is a bad one. If decisions are taken to maximize value for customers/investors by living/ not compromising the company values – the pit stop becomes a valuable stop.

GETTING INSPIRED FOR A BIGGER CAUSE

When people work on their individual goals, there is always a danger of forgetting the larger purpose towards which all are working. Aligning with the bigger purpose may at times mean that you sacrifice your individual goal so that one can achieve the team goal. If the team pit stop makes people realize this, it is a great team pit stop.

BONDING

Many people believe that you cannot have friends at the workplace. It is after all a competitive world. Be civil, but do not become friendly. This philosophy overlooks the fact that we are at our professional best with people who we trust. Hence team pit stops can also serve as opportunities for team members to bond with each other.

CELEBRATING

When you celebrate your team member's success, you own up his/her achievements. Taking pride in others' work is the first step in peer learning. Team pit stops that celebrate create positive energies and a sense of community.

CAPABILITY BUILDING

When a team considers multiple dimensions of an issue, it can take quality decisions. For example, a decision may involve the technical side, quality side, human side, financial side, legal side, values side, short term, long term and industry practices side to it. Ignoring any single side may affect the quality of the decision. Teams at times require capability building in some or all the dimensions. Team pit stops are great opportunities to build capabilities.

Self Reflect

Do your team pit stops contribute to

1. Collective Learning (able to connect the dots)

2. Problem solving (not problem fixing)

3. Getting inspired for a bigger cause (purpose alignment)

4. Celebrating (getting inspiration from each other's work)

5. Decision making (not safe decisions but right decisions)

6. Bonding (swim and sink together)

7. Capability Building (learning how to contribute towards making business successful)

If your team pit stops are not effective, conduct a health check of your team. This heath check lets you know at what stage of maturity your team is. If the team is in level 1 or 2 of maturity, it cannot conduct effective team pit stops. We will discuss this in the next section.

LAP 4 – SECTOR II

TEAM PIT STOP EFFECTIVENESS DIAGNOSTIC

Become your Team Doctor. Conduct Periodic Health Checks

WHERE IS YOUR TEAM RIGHT NOW?

Team pit stops are effective only when team members have the relevant collaboration skills and attitudes. As you read through the various stages of any team, reflect at what stage of maturity your team is right now and what you need to do to help the team to leverage the power of pit stops.

STAGE 1 - POLITE

Reflect on your interactions with fellow passengers during your train or air journey. If you are not one of those who considers everyone a long lost friend, is ready to give a warm hug and share stories of your childhood, you are likely to be formal, polite when you need to communicate and in general helpful. If your fellow passenger offers a point of view, you are very likely to listen, appear to be appreciative even if you do not agree. If someone were to take a video shoot of these interactions and show it to an audience, they may in fact assume that there is deep camaraderie between the two of you.

Of course, you know that's not true. There are no stakes. Hence there is no commitment. Hence there is general politeness.

Can you relate this to your interactions with some individuals or teams within your organization? Can you have an effective pit stop when the relationship is at this stage? There is hardly any trust between members. The pit stop at this stage can only be a formality or a less than honest communication exercise.

STAGE 2 - AT EACH OTHER'S THROAT

When people start working with each other – they need to provide leadership (take decisions) and also accept another's leadership (abide by another's decisions). There is a warrior in each one of us and we like to have our own small kingdoms at work. Warriors fight directly with other or through others.

Sometimes fighting takes the form of strategic non-cooperation like withholding resources and information.

When you chair your next meeting, step back and observe what is happening in the room. Is everyone enthusiastic? Are they talking to each other? Are they listening to each other? Are they giving and taking ideas from each other? Are the discussions issues based or are they getting personal with each other? Is the team expecting you to arbitrate or are they discussing differences and resolving them spontaneously? Are they having fun together or having fun at the cost of someone?

If the members are at each other's throat, the team cannot achieve much. In fact, many team leaders notice the dysfunctionalities but do not pay heed to them. Some leaders actually find it easy to manage a team that is in this stage as they constantly look up to the leader for taking decisions. Upward delegation from team members is delightful, especially for those leaders who do not know what else to do in their own job!

STAGE 3 – TRAFFIC RULES

Try this. If you find stage 2 behaviors in your team meetings, just state in plain words what you have observed without giving them the color of adjectives. Do not become judgmental. Then switch your mouth phone off or at least put it on a silent mode. This will make people talk. To begin with there will be a lot of discomfort. After that, someone will break the ice. This will set the group talking in an animated way. Just then, when you thought that the team was maturing, the smartest guy in your team will try to put a spanner in the works by saying, "We are wasting our time and we should get on with the task." This is the time to reactivate your mouth phone and tell the group that they are on the right track. It is time to have honest conversations. With your encouragement, someone will actually tell the smarty pants that he is the biggest problem in the team. Now hell will break lose. Sit back and watch but do not play politics. Let people talk, fight, accuse and pull each other's hair. They have been doing this all along either in their mind or behind each other's back. After a point they will have exhausted themselves and someone will say something magical like, "Hey, we are all at fault. We all need to change," or better still will own up and say, "I did not realize I have been causing so much pain. I am sorry." This is the turning point. You have to be patient to reach this summit of team evolution.

Then the team starts talking about norms that should govern their collective working- The Traffic Rules. The key here is to encourage the team to also decide on recognition for following traffic rules and punishments for violations. Leaders generally shy away from talking about punishments. It is important to let people know that membership into the team is not a position-based privilege; it is a right that needs to be earned.

STAGE 4 – THE ORCHESTRA

Think of what an orchestra conductor does during a concert. When he is moving the stick, he is not telling people what to play or when to play. Nobody is waiting for orders. Everyone is in a flow. What he represents is the vision of the music they are all playing. The orchestra conductor and the stick unify everyone into the beauty of the song. When your team is playing the orchestra, you through role modeling, energy and passion for the purpose ensure that the group becomes a high performance team. Your role is to take the team to the next level of performance. But what usually happens is that as the team starts working well together, following traffic rules, most managers happily retire as Review Managers. They move from meeting to meeting and review what others are doing and explain to their bosses what others are doing. Of course they also position it as their work. Remember that reviewing comes out of a need to ensure quality and is useful for a limited period when your team member is still learning. But how long will it be before the learning is over? How much time will it actually take before you start trusting him? If you have been reviewing someone who is in the role for a considerable period of time, it is important for you to ask the question- is the issue with that person or is it with you?

WHAT CAN YOU DO TO FACILITATE THE MOVEMENT OF YOUR TEAM FROM ONE STAGE TO THE NEXT?

What is the role you, as a leader, need to play at each stage of your team's evolution? What can you do to transition your team from where it is right now to stage four and beyond? Given below are some ideas. Just like your own health, you need to keep a close watch on your team's health. Changes within the team or outside, big or small, can impact the health of the team.

At stage 1　The group is at a forming stage when they initially come together. As strangers they are polite to each other. This could be mistaken as team harmony. The reality is they are not comfortable with each other, still testing waters and reluctant to disclose their feelings and expectations. The leader's job at this stage is to get them to know each other and feel comfortable with each other. Creating opportunities to interact without an agenda helps people to discover each other. This is also an important stage for sharing your vision and what values and behaviors constitute non-negotiable for you.

You would have done a great job as a leader if you got people to know each other's background and how that shaped them.

At stage 2　You have assigned roles to people and shared expectations. While each individual gets a role, they actually shape the role based on their understanding, talent, aspirations and working style. It is a blessing if you have more role shapers than role takers. However, the flip side is shapers have a personality of their own and that generally clashes with others with whom they need to work together. So you find that your team disintegrates into smaller like-minded groups. Instead of working together, they work within themselves and use you as the integrator to get work done. You may actually not mind this as you become a very important person in the new scheme of things. In fact you may promote, divide and rule as it works to your advantage. Unfortunately, it may not help you to realize the full potential of your team. As the team becomes dependent on you, you will find less time to focus on what will help you to grow and succeed in future. It's a lose-lose game.

So you need to decide to shift gears and surface conflicts. You should encourage transparency, respect and listening. You need to say no to being the arbitrator. You want people to deal with conflicts directly.

At stage 3 As people talk and become open, conflicts disappear. What takes its place is a deep understanding and affection for each other. This is a great time to collectively agree on the culture that the team wants and how to make each other accountable to live the culture and the common goal. The role of the leader at this stage is to be the process facilitator and to encourage the team to take charge of driving the culture.

At stage 4 Once there is bonding and accountability to each other, you as the leader can direct team energies towards the team goal. The team is now mature to work together, conduct effective planned and unplanned team pit stops and achieve high performance.

Many leaders directly jump to the last stage of directing energies without preparing the team. Hence most teams do not realize their true collective potential.

TEAM PIT STOP REFLECTION QUESTION

If your team meetings are your Pit Stops, do your team members take off after the pit stop?

Or crash land?

Before the meeting   During the meeting   After the meeting

Tense?   Defensive?   Burdened?

Team Pit Stops - Best Practices

Pit stops for team learning work well if the best available resources in the team coach others. AmEx formalized this process and is reaping benefits.

> At AmEx, team members are selected as Subject Matter Experts (SME). In this role they continue to be a part of their original functional teams and based on any future ramp-up, they are deputed as Shadow Trainers. In this capacity they are solely responsible for managing the learning curve of the learners assigned to them. They are also required to coach and regularly share feedback. At the end of the rotation the SMEs return to their team .

Similarly technology can enable great learning team pit stops.

Impromptu team pit stops can also develop deeper bonds and a sense of common purpose and community.

Small changes in the way we hold discussions can have a big impact

Edward De Bono's six thinking hats is a great method for promoting effective team decision-making. Generally when a solution for a problem or an opportunity is discussed, team members bring their own different points of view. Some may be in favor of certain things and others not in favor of the very same things. Some may have apprehensions and fears that they may not be able to substantiate or articulate sufficiently. Some may have concluded on the solution based on several untested assumptions. In such a situation, each member is trying to influence the other and generally, the meeting does not lead to any substantial output.

Edward De Bono has suggested a team based method of examining all dimensions of a solution. To begin with, all the team members wear a white hat and consider if they have all the facts necessary to take the decision. Then they all wear the yellow hat and think through the merits of the decision. Then they wear the black hat and think through the flip side/side effects of taking the decision. Then they wear the red hat and share gut level concerns. Then they wear the green hat and explore alternatives. By doing this, the team is able to take a well considered, debated and informed decision without letting biases and blinkers come in the way. It also helps in surfacing assumptions and premises that may not be well founded or data driven.

TEAM MEETING PIT STOPS FOR BUILDING CULTURE AND COMMUNITY

Employees spend 80-90% of their work time on their own role and work activities. Meetings are probably the only opportunity where they experience the organization at work. For example, take a sales person. 20-22 days in the month, the person is in the field and all by himself. Team review meetings that the person attends are probably the only occasion where the person experiences the organization. How you conduct the team meeting and what kind of cultural experience the person takes away from the meeting has a huge bearing on the impressions the person forms about your organization.

When a person comes to the office after 20 days of fieldwork, it is like homecoming. Do you give a hero's welcome to your sales executive? Is your interest only to see if the person has contributed to the monthly goal or is it also about the enhanced talent and understanding of the market that the person has acquired?

Do you also see the meeting as an opportunity for the person to feel connected with the larger organization? If yes, you would share the organizational achievements of the month and any developments that have a bearing on strategy, you make the person feel like a full member. If you use the team meeting to live each of the company values, you make the person live the organizational culture within the team meeting. The person will then become an ambassador of your organization.

LAP 4 – SECTOR III

HOW EFFECTIVE ARE YOUR UNPLANNED TEAM PIT STOPS?

Does a Team Tsunami bother you?

Conflict is a natural phenomenon in any team. Everyone has a way of thinking, communicating and working which could be irritating and intolerable to other team members. While teams are designed to collaborate, a healthy competitive spirit between team members is quite natural. Quite often this healthy spirit of competition can become not so healthy and team members may start becoming dysfunctional towards each other. Team storms are pit stops required to ensure that the team does not transcend into dysfunctional tsunami. This pit stop is to get a team back onto the high performance track by effectively dealing with the underlying tensions, team issues and break down in trusting relations.

While team storms appear to be a natural pit stop, it is interesting to observe how managers mess it up.

NOT HANDLING IS HANDLING

"After all the team members are adults. They are expected to deal with issues on their own. Anyways as long as the work gets done, why worry?"

These kinds of managers are task obsessed. For them nothing really merits a conversation other than real work. Maybe they are able to separate feelings from work and expect others also to do the same. To a large extent this works for all routine tasks expected of a work team. However, when it comes to non-routine situations, people who have issues with each other tend to draw boundaries and land up doing only their part of the work, as per written job guidelines. Due to this attitude customers suffer and the team may lose out on several opportunities. As most dissatisfied customers never speak (they just leave) the team manager may not even know the cost of poor intra team relationship. As far as lost opportunities are concerned, the team manager will get to know when some other team or competitor capitalizes on it.

Subtle handling

"Let's do an online peer to peer feedback or a team retreat or a workshop"

Here the manager acknowledges that there is a problem between the team members. However, he wants to use methods that are non-threatening. So he asks his HR function to organize an online peer-to-peer feedback (or an elaborate 360 degree feedback) and follow it up with a retreat at an exotic location. To begin with, HR would have to continuously follow up with the team members to get them to fill in their feedback forms about each other. Generally, people fill these forms on the last date of the second extension! The clique groups use the online feedback forms to celebrate each other. People who do not like each other either take this opportunity to slap each other by clicking on 1 out of 5 on a five-point scale or a diplomatic 3. The qualitative feedback people give each other is either too generic or too pedantic or clouded with hidden agendas. The individual reports are shared with the concerned team member. The overall summary of the strengths and weaknesses of the team are presented in the retreat.

At the retreat, consultants generally use structured exercises to help team members learn their orientation as team members and how they deal with each other in difficult situations. Some learning happens. Consultants also encourage feedback to each other. That also is in general useful. The team and members within the team make team vision and action plans. They make grandiose commitments about becoming a great team. Then they all come back and life moves on as usual.

Teams that get addicted to retreats keep repeating the cycle every year.

If only the manager had sought a team meeting and stated honestly the games that team members were playing, if only he called their bluff – the team would have transitioned into an authentic team.

SUBVERSIVE HANDLING

Talking behind the back

Managers who talk about their team members behind their back are those who do not have the courage to do so face to face with the concerned and cannot keep their emotional distress to themselves. In life nothing that one speaks remains confidential. It reaches the concerned person but through a third person in a spiced up manner. Some clever managers think that this is a smart way of letting the person know. In their mind this is non-threatening to the person as well as themselves. However, talking behind others' back erodes trust, creates an environment of gossip and backbiting. Sadly the real issue stays unresolved and assumes greater proportions over time.

AGGRESSIVE HANDLING

Enforcing non-negotiable team behaviors.

At time, managers want to make it amply clear and do not want to leave anything to chance or misinterpretation. They also want things to change immediately. While sharing non-negotiable team behaviors is a great thing to do, the way it is done matters equally. Aggressiveness leads to temporary alignment of the team members with what the leader wants; it does not result in awareness and awakening.

BEST WAYS TO HANDLE TEAM STORMS

END MEETINGS WITH A PROCESS CHECK

A simple question, such as what went well, and what needs improvement, at the end of each meeting provides great feedback on how the team is managing its pit stop and surfaces issues that could then be explored and resolved.

SURFACE CONFLICTS USING GLADS, SADS AND MADS

Have a zero hour in every team meeting wherein any issue troubling team members can be brought out. Ask each team member to write down what about the way they work they are glad about, sad about and mad about. Members can write this on cards. The cards are collected, shuffled and read out. This ensures anonymity, and at the same time surfaces conflicts. Our experience is once the issues are surfaced; team members realize that several others also share the same pain areas. This leads to open dialogue and resolution of the conflicts.

GOING BACK TO PURPOSE AND NORMS

Once in a while teams should reflect on the extent to which they are living the team purpose and norms. We all connect with a bigger purpose. If it is done in a participative manner, a common purpose bonds the team members together. If norms of working together are created in the context of the purpose, members see the value of following team rules. Going back periodically to reflect on team purpose and norms is a useful pit stop to keep alive a community spirit as well as the hunger to succeed.

At this stage you might be wondering if there are any interesting practices that companies adopt to make their unplanned team pit stops effective. This is the focus of the next section.

LAP 4 – SECTOR IV

BEST PRACTICES TO MAKE UNPLANNED TEAM PIT STOPS EFFECTIVE

BEST PRACTICES

CONFLICT MANAGEMENT TRAINING AT GENENTECH

Genentech offers all employees training titled "Crucial Conversations" on how to express themselves, as well as on how to listen successfully to each other. This training helps people to deal with conflict situations effectively, without compromising on their relationships with each other. In a way the training helps their employees to learn how to discuss their differences with respect to ideas, values and ways of working to arrive at win-win outcomes.

COME TO JESUS AT SOUTHWEST

Conflicts are a fact of life. Instead of viewing conflicts as a destructive force, Southwest uses them constructively to build relationships and improve performance. The company is very proactive in identifying and resolving conflicts.

To resolve conflicts, Southwest has a well-defined process:

1. The parties themselves are encouraged to use every means available to first resolve the conflict themselves.. If that's not possible, managers are expected to take an active role in developing a solution, which will be suitable.

2. An information-gathering meeting is held, at which both sides of the conflict put forward their perspectives on the issues involved. Many times, conflicts sort themselves out at this stage mainly because better communication is achieved.

3. If the conflict is still unresolved, the managers hold what is called unofficially a "Come to Jesus" meeting. This is a face-to-face meeting, which takes an entire day. By the end of this meeting, most problems have been resolved because of the dialogue that takes place between the parties and the managers.

The overall process sounds simple, but when well implemented, conflict resolution can become more of a team building exercise and less of a source of destructive energy. Note that Southwest takes a proactive approach to resolving disputes, and never leaves these conflicts and differences as background issues, which should be ignored. Instead, the company works on the premise that conflicts will naturally arise from time to time – particularly given the pressures of the flight schedule an airline works to. But by using these conflicts productively, as opportunities for learning, Southwest strengthens relationships between groups of employees, shares knowledge and fosters mutual respect between different teams within the company.

USING REAL STORIES TO PROMOTE THE NON-NEGOTIABLE WAY TO DEAL WITH TEAM CONFLICTS

Every new employee at Eicher would hear a story about handling conflicts with team members. The story went something like this -

"One day a direct reportee of Vikram Lal came to him and started criticizing his peer. Lal called up that peer and asked his direct reportee to now speak in front of him what he does not appreciate about him. This story is part of Eicher Bible; lesson on conflict handling, which are not supposed to be violated, come what may. You simply cannot bitch about your colleague. If you truly care, you speak to the person directly and deal with what is bothering you."

Stories are the truths that team members experience in an organization. People do not connect with speeches, preaching, and exhortations on team conduct. They connect with real stories of what has been appreciated and condemned in the past. Hence promote existing stories of non-negotiable ways to deal with team conflicts. Also work towards creating new stories.

In the previous sections, we have explored organizational and team pit stops. Let's now dig deeper into the individual pit stops. This is the theme for the remaining sections of this book.

LAP 5
INDIVIDUAL PIT STOPS

Lap 5 – Sector 1

Are you the clown in your annual appraisal circus?

Is your annual performance review pit stop a Feedback of last year

or

A Feed Forward for the next year's strategy?

You must have played a fun game called free word association. I am going to put some words up to you. You have to call out whatever you associate them with. Better still, what do you think your team members will associate these words with? Being spontaneous is important. There are obviously no right or wrong answers. Take up one word at a time and call out whatever you associate the word with.

Fun

Future

Appraiser

Rating

Bell Curve

Performance Appraisal

Appraisee

Appraisal Discussion

Development Planning in performance appraisal

Your word associations would be directly related to your past experiences or what you have heard from others within your current organization or past organizations. If the direct or indirect experiences were positive, your word association images would reflect that. However for many people the experiences of annual performance appraisal are negative. Thinking of performance appraisal provokes anger in most people. For many, performance appraisal conversations represent the best of what is worst about HR in the organization. In a research conducted by Right Management India on causes for attrition, poor handling of performance appraisal has been cited as the topmost reason for people leaving the organization.

As a Manager, do you consider yourself as a victim of a bad process or as contributor to how the process is practiced in your organization?

Use these reflection statements to think. These statements depict behaviors and attitudes of appraisers in the appraisal process. It is never a black and white situation. Just tick what largely represents you. If you are not a manager, reflect on how managers in your organization handle the annual appraisal meeting pit stop.

Appraisal Pit Stop	Tick
I get into an appraisal meeting without gathering performance data about the individual.	
I think appraisal serves largely as an administrative activity with not much impact.	
I withhold giving feedback until the end of year.	
I rarely find opportunities to congratulate my team members on their achievements throughout the year.	
I give generic feedback.	
I avoid giving specific feedback on poor performance.	
I do not share my feedback on KRAs with my appraisees.	
I interrupt a lot when my appraisees talk during the appraisal meeting.	
Addressing the development plan of my appraisees is primarily the responsibility of the HR. My job is to follow up to ensure completion.	
The development plan of my appraisees largely comprises of classroom training.	

If your answer is a decisive YES to most of the statements, you are messing up with appraisal as an effective pit stop.

WHY DO WE NEED ANNUAL APPRAISAL PIT STOP AT ALL?

Does it sometimes occur to you whether we need this pit stop at all? Some of us may feel, "Why do you need this annual appraisal pit stop at all? After all, this is such a waste of time, an HR exercise that has no relevance at all?"

Let's explore this question.

Imagine you are the manager of a team member whose responsibility is to carry heavy weights. The person is literally expected to carry a heavy bag of weight from one point to the other - several times during the day and every day of the year.

Your target for the next year has doubled. Now you need to load this person further.

Any further load on this guy's back and he is going to give in. Or maybe not, if you support him by taking part of his load. But who will do your work, if you start doing your team member's work?

The only way your team member will be able to do a great job of the next year's work on his own is if he can think creatively. That can happen only if he and you have a discussion on what can be improved in the way the team member handled the work in the previous year. The improvement discussion will generate new ideas, and when the manager supports the team member in implementing those ideas, you will see significant improvement in the performance.

A sample creative idea to carry heavier load effortlessly.

You need time to think creatively and unblock hidden potential. Hence time for reflection. This is precisely what is expected of an annual appraisal conversation. Use the past year's experience to feed forward learning and ideas for the next year.

You probably hold such conversations throughout the year. Hence you may feel that in your case an annual appraisal discussion may not be required. However, the time of annual appraisal also coincides with the start of the next financial year. This means new organizational and departmental goals have to be set. Probably these are significantly more challenging than the previous year. This implies that every employee has to discover the hidden potential to perform at a significantly higher level of excellence. Discovering hidden potential has to be in the context of the next year's goals. Only then does the organization start scoring from the first month of the next financial year, and doing it in an effortless manner.

Let's say a few managers in your organization do not conduct performance appraisal conversations. Do you realize how this seemingly insignificant action can have a far-reaching impact on your business performance and growth? You would have realized by now that annual appraisal pit stop is not a good to do thing but a must to do thing. Now the question is how to conduct the annual appraisal pit stop in a manner that is effective. This is the point of reflection in the next section.

LAP 5 – SECTOR II

THE LEGENDARY STORY OF A GOOD AND BAD APPRAISAL PIT STOP

Given below are two different appraisal pit stop conversations. Reflect on what behaviors of the appraiser contribute to an effective appraisal pit stop? Which of the following mirror your behavior as an appraiser?

Aisa Hi Hota Hai (It happens this way only)

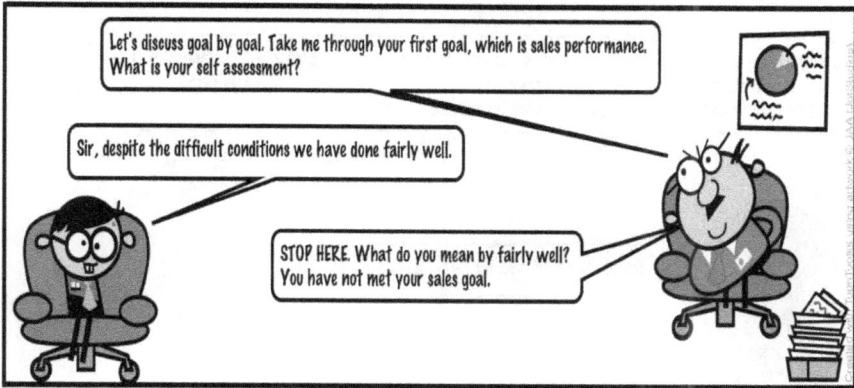

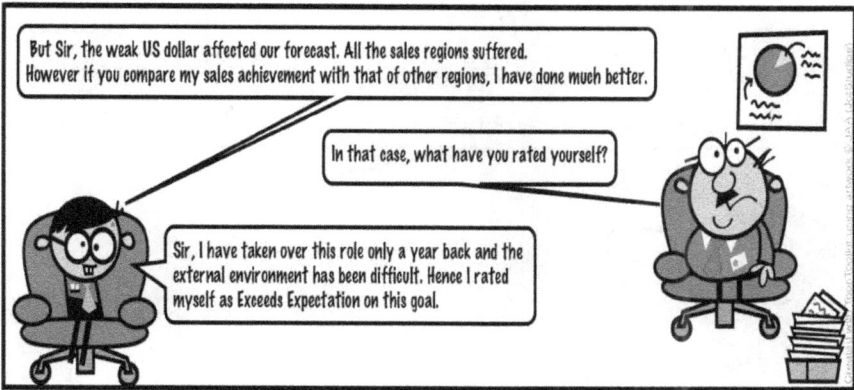

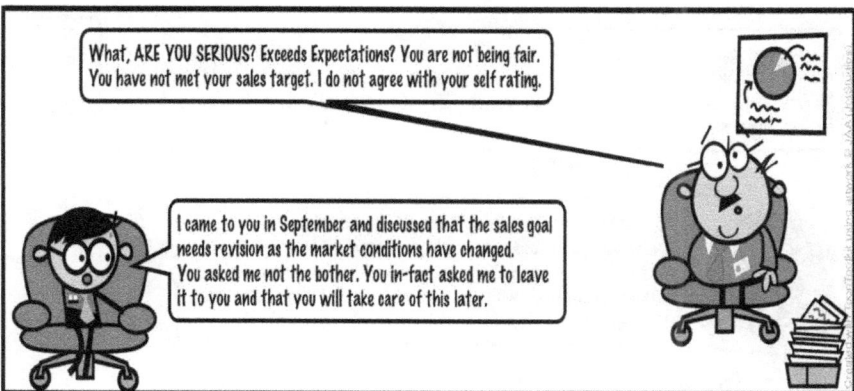

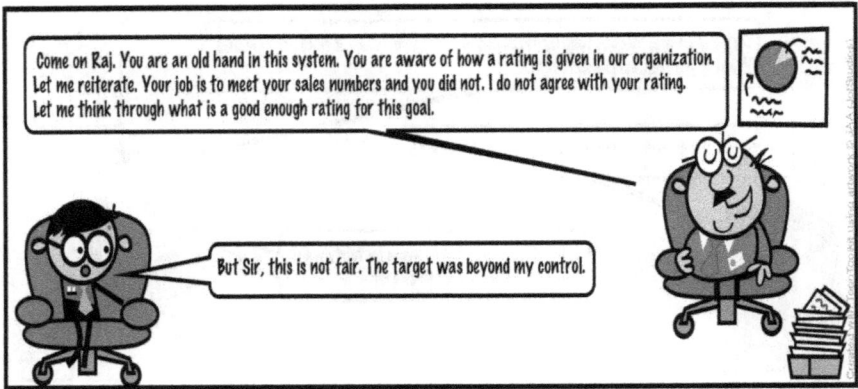

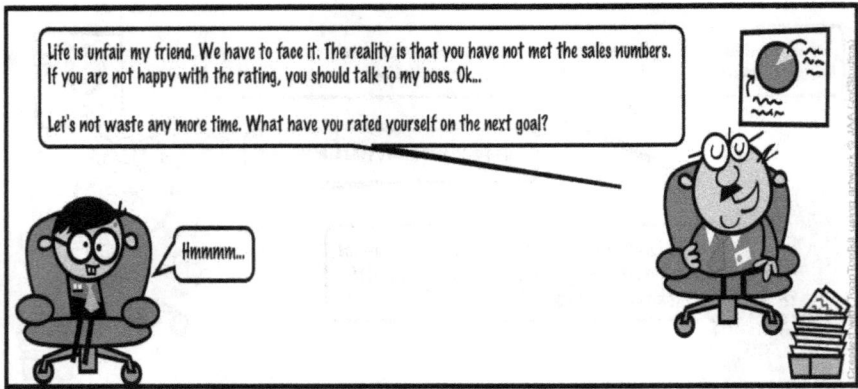

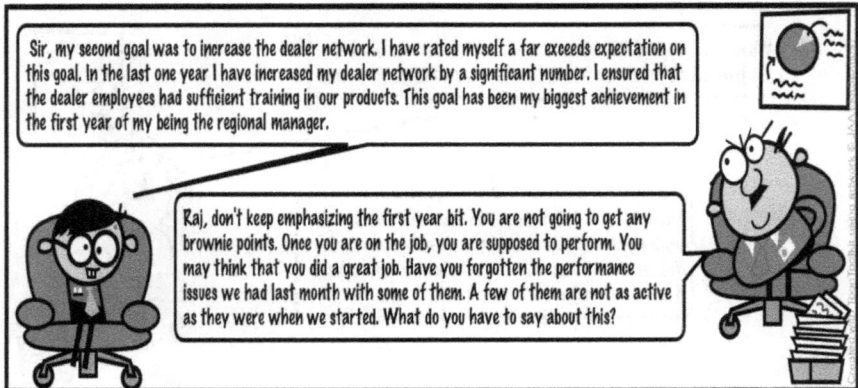

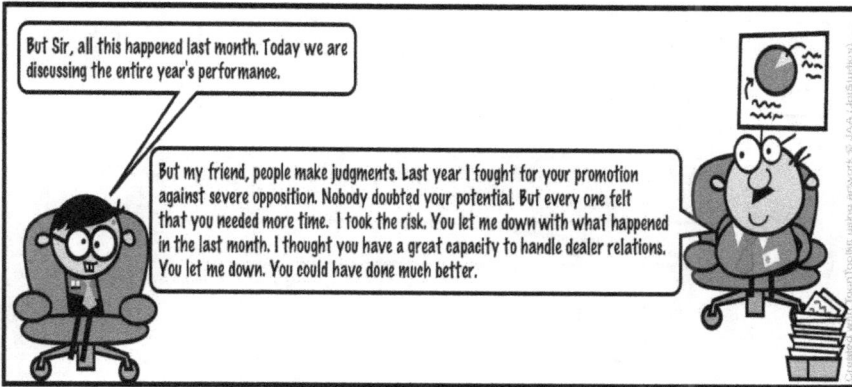

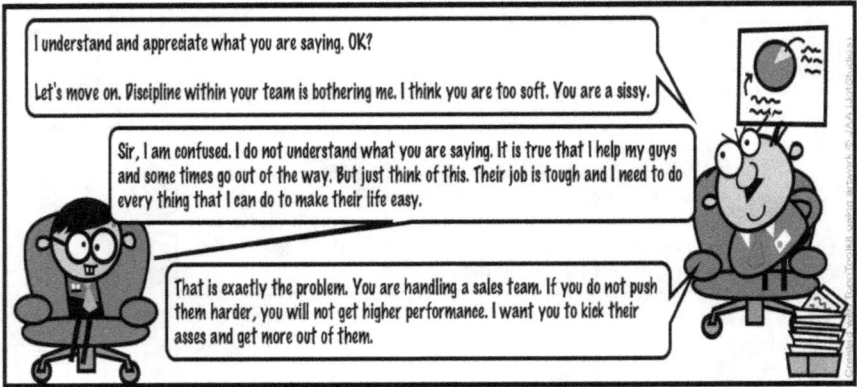

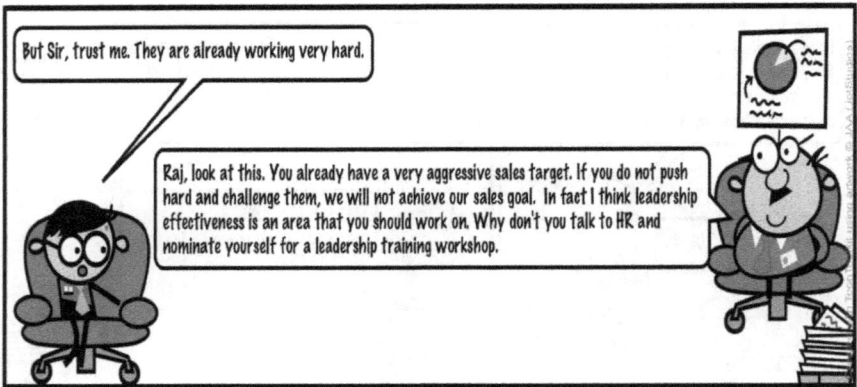

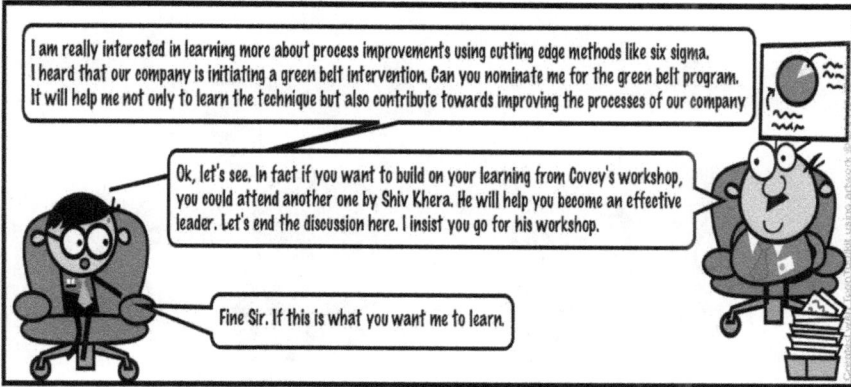

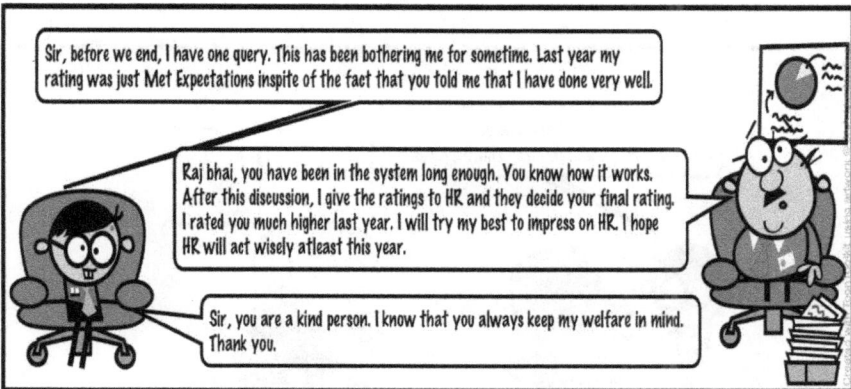

Aisa Bhi Ho Sakta Hai
(It can also happen this way)

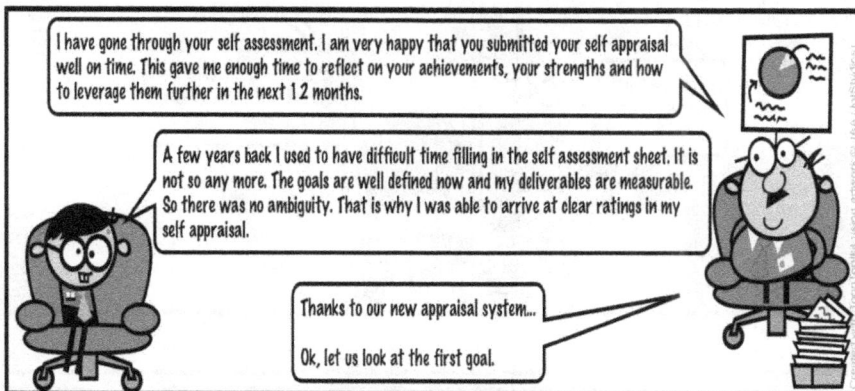

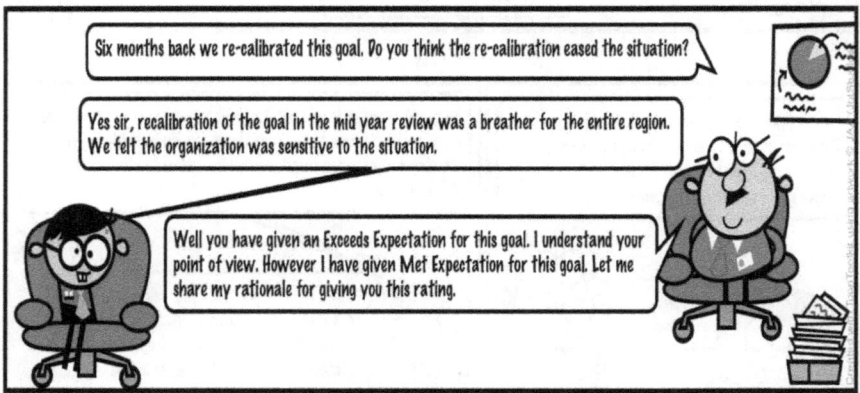

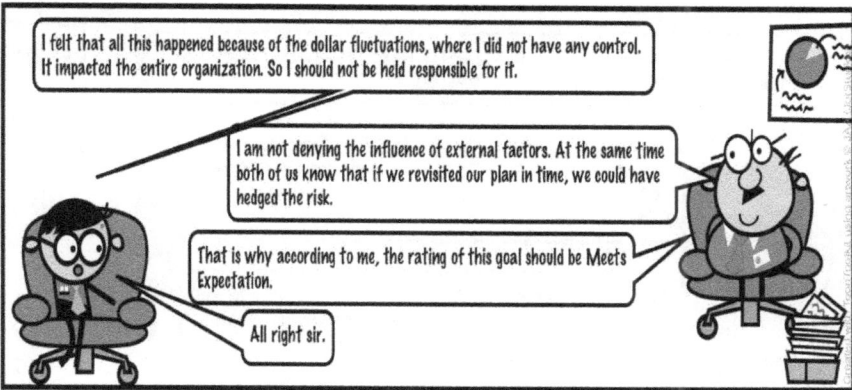

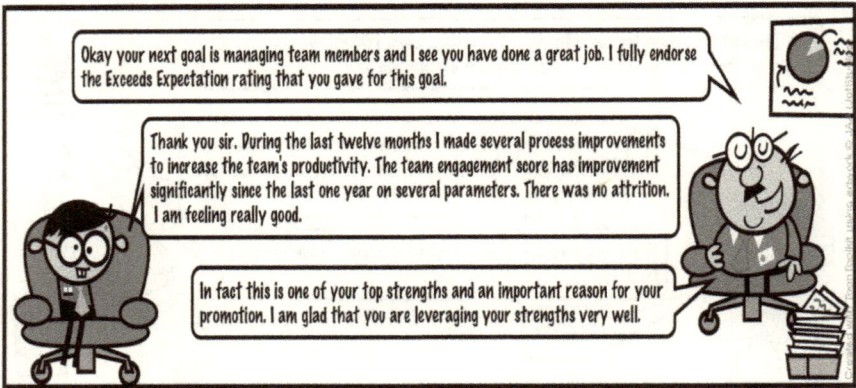

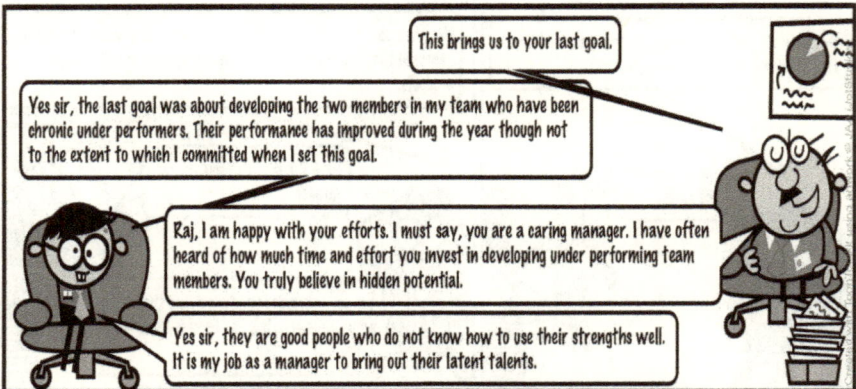

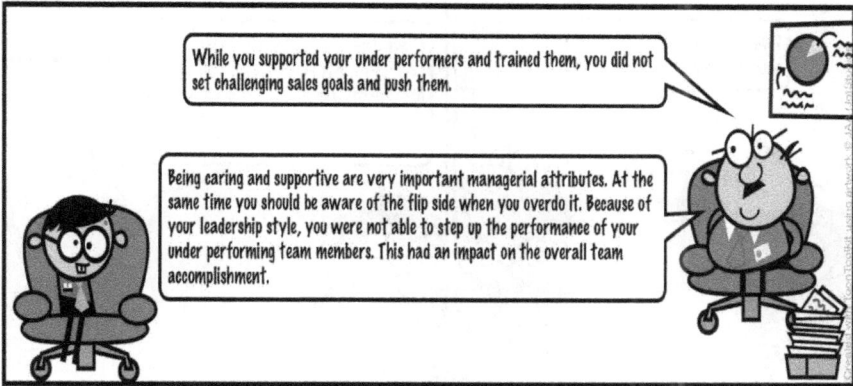

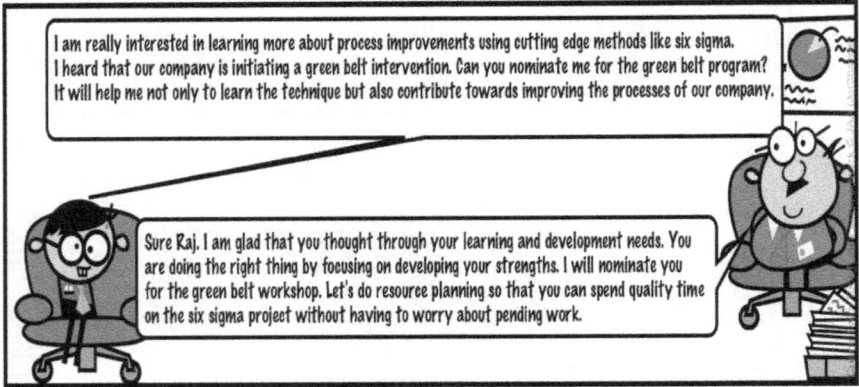

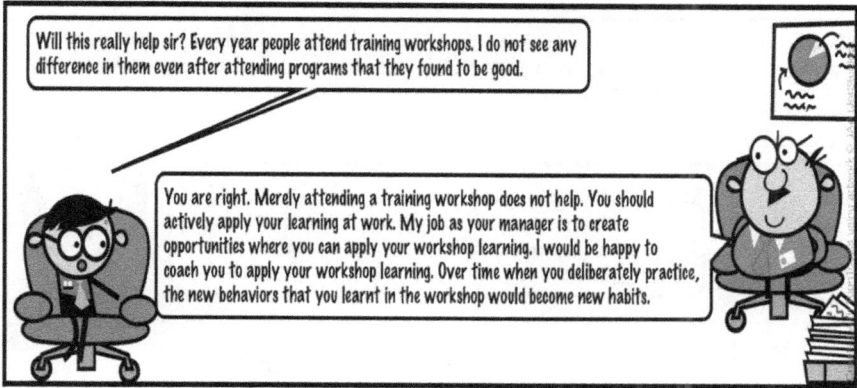

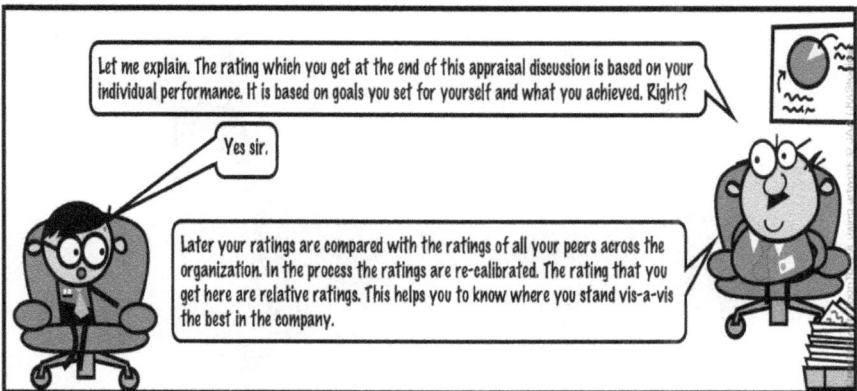

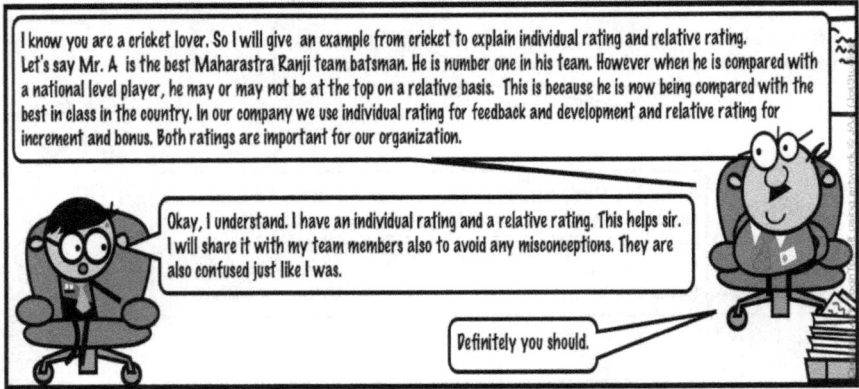

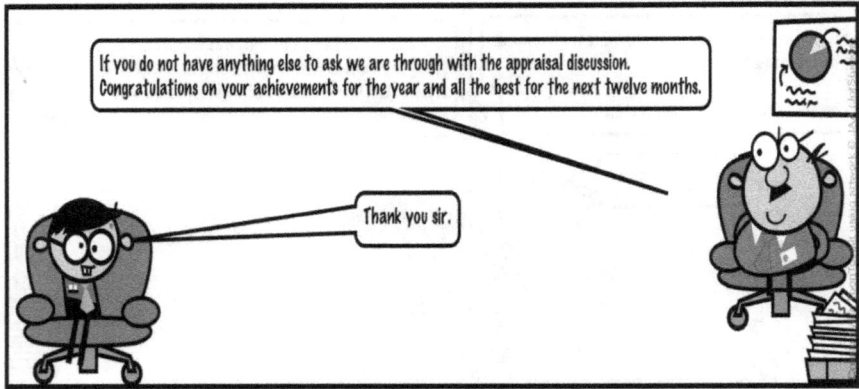

The 15-minute conversation

Is the annual appraisal meeting with your team members a 15-minute conversation that you conduct in your office when you have another half a dozen things that are in your mind? If this is the case it is better you do not conduct the meeting rather than go through the motions of this farcical exercise.

Your HR would probably conclude that this is a development issue. They may organize a training workshop on how to conduct appraisal meetings. You will learn how to demonstrate listening, care, empathy, give feedback and help the person to discover their hidden potential. Between handling emails and calls on your cell phone, you will pick up all that is important for you to do an effective job of an appraiser.

Then you will go back and do exactly what you do best – a 15 minute conversation.

Let's say just before you had planned the usual 15-minute conversation, a customer or a client came to your office. The first thing you would do is to greet them heartily, making it amply clear that the customer is the most important person for you. You then put your cell phone on silent mode and tell your secretary that you should not be disturbed and he should handle any calls that may come in. You will then give a broad smile to your customer, lean forward and become ready to listen to what the person wants to say. You empathize with the person's situation and concerns. You take notes, paraphrase what the person said and ensure that you understood the person correctly. Wherever you have a different view, you put it in a respectful manner that contributes to a constructive conversation. You do all this because you know that the customer is the person who will help you and your company become successful. You have the attitude and skills to build customer relations.

But then doesn't your team member also do the same thing? Help you and your organization to become successful? How come you are reluctant to use the skills that you demonstrated in ample measure with your customer, with your team members? The answer is that most managers simply do not care. Team members are disposable tools for their success. If a tool is broken, throw it away and seek a new tool. The same is with a team member. Managers who feel this way may find even a 15-minute appraisal conversation with their team member a waste of time.

Reflect on your attitudes towards team members and how they manifest in the annual appraisal pit stop. Do you see a need for building greater trust through the appraisal conversations? If yes, here are some ideas.

BUILDING TRUST THROUGH THE APPRAISAL CONVERSATIONS

If the annual appraisal has to be an effective pit stop, managers have to provide feedback to their employees throughout the year. Normally feedback is psychologically associated with what the person has to improve. This is one of the reasons why team members become defensive in receiving feedback and managers have discomfort in giving feedback.

Let's redefine the way feedback is given so that it builds trust and also contributes to high performance.

Would you agree that every person, along with their weaknesses has some core strengths? Let's say a person is living her strength to the fullest. Is it possible that any strength taken to a level of excellence creates a corresponding weakness?

For example, if logic is your strength, you may want to win every argument using impeccable logic. You may in the process forget that there is an emotional side to the issue. Let's say your team member is upset that he has not got promotion and shares her feelings about this with you. You are very clear that she is not yet ready for the promotion. Try dealing with the situation by offering her your perfect logic on why she didn't deserve the promotion. You will lose the person. Give her time to share her emotions. She will feel better and get on with life.

Similarly, while we all suffer because of our weaknesses, their flip side is also a strength that accompanies it. For example your inability to say no may be causing your boss and other colleagues to dump their work on you. But the good will and trust this builds may result in career growth or may result in significant diversification of your own skills.

Your role in an appraisal pit stop is to give feedback on the person's strengths and how to handle the flip side effectively. When you approach feedback in this manner your team member can see you helping her to become successful. This builds trust. Instead, if it is a mechanical strength weaknesses feedback, it only makes the person defensive. That apart, it will not help the person or the organization to be a winner.

Celebrating Strengths and discussing how the flip side of the strength can be addressed demonstrates your respect for the team member.

Several companies use elaborate online feedback surveys as a tool to know if employees are happy with their appraisal experience. At the core there is only one question to ask.

Did the employee experience the process to be fair?

The answer would be either Yes or No.

The top 25 companies in the Great Place to Work Survey every year score high on the parameter of fairness. The way they handle the performance appraisal process to a large extent contributes to this employee feedback. The question here is what contributes to the perception of unfairness? We want to raise a few questions for you to reflect as an appraising manager.

QUESTION 1: ARE YOU LISTENING TO THE STORY TELLER?

By nature managers are interested only in outcomes – if an employee was given a task, did she accomplish it or not? However, an employee would be interested in sharing the story of how she went about dealing with the challenges she faced and how smartly she navigated the process to accomplish the task. She might hate giving away the outcome without sharing the plot. Just like a novel. The excitement of the novel comes from dramatizing the story, not by summarizing the story and outcome in five lines.

For each KRA, an employee has put in efforts through the year. The efforts may have created high or low impact. Nevertheless, the employee has put in effort. Appraisal pit stop is a time when the warrior comes home to share the adventure. As a manager, if you do not show interest and worse still get restless and reprimand him or her for telling you stories, you are missing out on the basics of human psychology.

When you listen to the story keenly, you will also get to know the company values and competencies that the person has demonstrated. When people achieve high performance, they are in a flow. They may not even realize in entirety what enabled their success. So when you listen to the story, you can help the person to become aware of his and her own strengths. This would help him to replicate his success in future as well.

QUESTION 2: IS IT YOUR TEAM MEMBER'S SHOW TIME?

Be honest. Through the year you were talking and your team member was listening. Appraisal time is an un-interrupted space for the person to talk. It's his show time. Be the audience; do not try to grab that space. Let your team member be the hero.

People in organizations are dying to be heard. The way organizations and the notion of hierarchy is structured, seniors are expected to talk and tell and juniors are expected to listen and do. By and large this is how your company may be operating. If not, you are part of a minority.

Maybe listening to your team member does not come easily to you. After all, she is not as smart or intelligent as you. For that one-hour why not think of this person as a customer of your company, or maybe an investor in the company. Or else think of that one-hour as a paid workshop that you are attending;

and you are listening to a well-known trainer. We listen to our customers, investors and external consultants keenly even if they are talking utter nonsense. Why can't we do the same with our own team members?

Question 3: Are there BIG Surprises?

When team members share that the manager's feedback in the annual appraisal came as a big unpleasant surprise, it may not automatically mean that the Manager has not been giving regular feedback. In fact, many managers do give feedback throughout the year. It could well be that the team member did not care enough to take them seriously. Through the year let's say you gave your team member who handles training an improvement feedback that he should be better planned. You may have given this feedback when there was some problem. When people are feeling low, when they experience failure they are very likely to take feedback without contesting or exploring real issues. However, the same person may not agree to the feedback in a high stake conversation. Hence it is useful to give feedback in terms of effect rather than the cause. In the above case the cause is poor planning, the effect is very few participants in workshops, and hence low impact and high per participant cost of training. Sharing effect makes the person think about how to work towards addressing the problem rather than become defensive about his competency.

Question 4: Is your feedback just a summary of your team member's strengths and weaknesses?

As managers we tend to expect all competencies in every employee and also look at each competency in isolation. Whereas an organization is a collective of people who between them demonstrate the competencies required for the organization to become successful. Expecting each person to be an epitome of all the competencies is like demanding that every employee turn into Superman. Similarly each individual's talent is not a sum of competencies. It is the way the person applies the competencies.

Hence the strengths and weaknesses applied together create an individual's talent. For example my strength is being innovative. My weakness is being too accommodative. If a manager gives me improvement feedback in a conventional way, he would ask me to be assertive. However, my weakness actually enhances my strength. Because I am too accommodative, I take every feedback seriously and look at how to apply it to create a better solution. Actually, being too accommodative is a weakness if I was not innovative. Innovation and accommodation create a talent that makes me who I am. Hence traditional feedback frameworks surprise people and may be even self defeating. Share the effect, share examples and help the person explore how to become effective. This will make the person feel that you are being fair to him.

QUESTION 5: DO YOU DIFFERENTIATE THOSE WHO PERFORM WELL?

How do you treat people who perform well? Giving them good ratings is not good enough. You should clearly communicate that you value them by giving honest ratings to those who have not performed well. Several managers want to be nice with employees. Hence, they tend to give moderate ratings to underperforming employees. For high performing employees fairness is the relative difference between the ratings that they got in comparison to what average and underperforming employees have been given.

QUESTION 6: ARE YOU DATA BASED DURING THE APPRAISAL DIALOGUE?

Being data based is not about coming up with quantitative evidence. It is about sharing actions and the impact of those actions on business. When managers give feedback on a KRA in isolation, it is not being data based, even if the feedback is a SMART feedback. For example, aggression can be both a strength and weakness depending on the context; at the same time any behavior- in this case aggression- rarely occurs as an isolated phenomenon. It is attached to a string of other related behaviours. For example, in the example above aggression may be accompanied by disrespectful language or lack of willingness to listen- hence offering feedback that the person needs to work on her/ his aggression has to positioned in a context; at the same time other behaviours which may be attached to this one behavior may also have to be shared, to explain what the person needs to work on. Sharing data means thinking of the 'Big picture' – looking at a situation from above and viewing clusters of behaviours that work together in affecting high performance.

QUESTION 7: IS "WHAT DID YOU DO BEYOND THE KEY RESULT AREAS' A PET QUESTION THAT YOU ASK YOUR APPRAISEES?

At times, managers ask this question to employees in their appraisal conversation:

"What did you do beyond the KRAs? If you just accomplished your KRAs you have met expectations. If you have done more than your KRAs, you have exceeded expectations."

This is an erroneous perception. Key Result Areas of individuals are derived out of the departmental KRAs and they in turn emerge out of the organizational KRAs. Key Result Areas by definition are that that will have the biggest impact on the company's performance and growth. They are like your 20 in the 80:20 of Pareto (20% of activities have 80% impact on the outcome). So if a person focuses solely on the KRAs, he/she is being wise. In fact, everyone in the organization should give disproportionate time and energies on the KRAs. Hence if a person accomplished her KRAs, the person has demonstrated excellence and not average performance.

QUESTION 8: DO YOU VALUE THOSE WHO LIVE BY THE RULES OF COMPANY VALUES?

Let's say collaboration is a company value. This means that employees are expected to live this value consistently in their behavior and actions. Let's say your team member has exceeded expectation on a KRA. However, the person has not lived out this value in achieving this KRA. Will you still give the person exceeds expectation or would you discount the performance? Most companies have appraisal systems where KRAs and Values are rated separately. KRA achievement is seen as an indicator of high performance.

While values shape the long-term identity and reputation of the firm, their impact on the present is not so evident. For example, collaboration may actually delay things in the present while it may strengthen the quality of a long-term decision. However, what is evident and measurable is the delay in decision-making. Thus, not living your values may hasten decision-making and get you instant rewards but in the long run it may have serious negative effects. Of course, one can take heart from the fact that for every Rajat Gupta who is caught, many get away. You are probably one of those lucky ones to have escaped punishment.

The nice thing is most of us want to live by the rules – one of the fallouts of domestication by our parents, teachers and society. However, there are outliers and these could unfortunately be the high performers of your organization. So how do you handle a situation where taking short cuts and not following values consistently is the mindset of your smart high performer?

QUESTION 9: BLAME THE RELATIVE RATING ON HR

If there is anything that ticks off managers about annual appraisals, it is relative rating. Managers feel that relative ranking is outside the individual's control and hence is not fair.

This logic is far from the truth.

Let me take an example from your personal life. If your child is smart and does well in school, what do you do to ensure that he/she does not become complacent? You encourage your child to go for Olympiads where he/she would know the meaning of excellence and where one is pitted against other equally smart children. This is the way you would prepare your child to face greater competition. Does the same logic not hold good for your team? Is it important for you and your team members to know where the person stands vis-à-vis peers across the company? Relative rating is all about this.

You may say, how can one compare your team member who belongs to a function with a peer who belongs to another function? While the work is functional, the role is the same. A manager's role for instance is to manage, irrespective of the department. Importantly, the goal of both these role holders is the same – to ensure effective execution of strategy within their team. Accepting relative rating does not come easy, especially if you talk about it only during the annual appraisal meeting. Build an orientation within your team wherein team members regularly reflect on these questions "How are my KRAs impacting the organization's strategy and goals" and "What more can I do with respect to my KRAs so that I can impact the organization's strategy and goals?" They then would be appreciative of their relative ratings.

Before you turn the page, reflect on each of these questions

1. As an appraiser, where do you need to change your orientation?

2. What do you need to do, to stop the 15-minute appraisal drama?

LAP 5 – SECTOR III

ASKING QUESTIONS AND GIVING FEEDBACK–THE
ART AND SCIENCE OF APPRAISAL PIT STOP

Go Prepared with Questions not Answers

If your objective as an appraiser is to make the person think and become more capable, an appraisal conversation is a wonderful platform. To make a person to think, you cannot give answers. You have to ask smart questions that help the person to think.

I have a few indicative questions you may find interesting:

Indicative questions that an appraiser can use	
Question	**Rationale**
How do you feel about your performance during the last 12 months?	Gives you a sense of the appraisee's energies, motivation levels & expectations so that you can moderate the dialogue accordingly.
Can you please take me through how you went about each goal/KRA and what has been the measurable impact? Can you please take me through how you applied company competencies and company values in the achievement of your goals?	Mitigates possibilities of exposing the organization to risk if the company values are not followed. It also provides the appraisee with an opportunity to find unrealized potential by applying the competencies that he/she has not yet applied in the future.

What are the strengths that you discovered in yourself?	Gives you an opportunity to appreciate the appraisee's strengths. Also creates awareness about which skills the appraisee should use more of. You can also give feedback on how they can be leveraged further.
What is the opportunity for you to improve your performance? Or What is the block that, if removed, could improve your performance?	Creates awareness about the improvement areas for the appraisee so that he/she can identify his/her hidden potential.
Give me feedback about the quality of management support I provided? What more could I have done?	Gives the appraisee an opportunity to give feedback to you w.r.t. your leadership style - strengths and improvement areas.
What future roles and responsibilities do you aspire to take up?	Helps you to understand the appraisee's aspirations that can be leveraged upon to create a plan that suits both organizational and individual needs. Also builds trust and respect in your relationship.

Asking the right questions is 50% of the job well done. The remaining 50% consists of giving effective feedback. Effectiveness in giving feedback is more than just skills. It is about being authentic. Feedback is a great opportunity to demonstrate authenticity. Trust is built when you are authentic. I am going to present to you two feedback situations. I would like you to reflect which feedback builds trust and which does not.

Situation 1   Pranita is a customer sales representative who has performed exceedingly well. She gets feedback in her annual appraisal:

1. Pranita you've exceeded the target by 130%. Let's see how you do next year.

2. Pranita, you've exceeded the target by 130%! Congratulations.

3. Pranita, the corporate promotion event you lead has made 130% target possible. I must congratulate you on this!

4. Pranita, the corporate promotion event you lead has made 130% target possible. I think your interpersonal skills and in-depth product knowledge are outstanding. You have proven yourself to be a valuable asset to our organization.

5. Pranita, the corporate promotion event you lead has made 130% target possible even in this unfavourable market scenario. Your interpersonal skills and in-depth product knowledge are outstanding. Our customers are delighted as is clear in the client satisfaction survey. You have proven yourself to be a valuable asset to our organization in these times of slowdown.

Situation 2   Anand is a high performer, but has poor interpersonal skills. He gets feedback in the appraisal meeting

1. Anand, your rough behavior with your colleagues is unacceptable.

2. Anand, I have observed that you behave in a rough manner sometimes. You perform well, but are poor at managing work relationships.

3. I don't understand why you behave in a rough manner with your peers Anand. It's not right. You should be respectful and mindful of their feelings.

4. I have noticed that you tend to lose temper when in a tough situation. This makes the situation worse. While you get the job done, it leaves a bad feeling with your colleagues. They fear your temper and tend to hide bad news until it becomes a major crisis. This in turn creates tougher situations for you.

In Situation 1, the first feedback seem to be matter of fact. There is no appreciation. It is data-based and proclaimed with skepticism. It seems as if the manager does not believe that this performance can be repeated- a clear care of distrust. The second feedback will make the team member feel good. As the feedback focuses on the result that the team member has achieved, and not on the behaviors that the person has demonstrated (unless the team member is aware of or specifically asks for feedback about her behaviour), she will not be able to do any thing with the feedback except feel good about it. When a person understands what behaviors she has demonstrated and how these behaviors have contributed to the result, she is likely to use then actively and build on them for greater success. This behavior-impact connection is noticeable in the third and the fourth feedbacks. The last feedback in Situation 1 also gives the context in which the person demonstrated specific behaviors and achieved success.

Similarly in Situation 2 except the fourth feedback, all other feedbacks are not effective. Feedback number four captures the context, behavior and impact. The person will understand what one needs to do to turnaround performance and succeed. Hence if you want to build trust, this is the most apporiate way of giving improvement feedback.

CONVERTING KNOWLEDGE INTO AWARENESS – THE REAL VALUE OF FEEDBACK

Just think about it. There are four reactions to any feedback.

WHY THIS KOLAVARI?

Does it happen at times that when a person gives feedback, you wonder, is there more to this? In my first organization, whenever

I would heartily appreciate my team members they would know that some big workload was round the corner. Does this happen to you? I mean do people become wary when you give feedback – whether it is positive or improvement related?

PUZZLED

If you give this feedback - "I think you are doing a great job. Just keep it up," what should your team member make of it? If he were an optimistic person he would assume that this is about the results or some behaviors that he/she is producing If he were a pessimistic person, he would conclude that he has got the best recognition for the year and should not expect anything more (like a promotion etc.). The phrase 'doing a great job' is like a lost symbol that only Dan Brown can decipher.

PAPA DON'T PREACH

How often do we get feedback that we already know – good, bad and ugly? Why do people keep repeating the same thing? It is irritating. But wait a minute. How come we have difficulty in changing even though we know what we have to change? Knowing is probably not equal to awareness. Let me explain the difference between knowing and awareness, using a common phenomenon among students in India. Many students mug up their textbooks. They can put down what they have memorized very effectively when writing the exam. But do they really understand what they have mugged up? Maybe not. Awareness is all about understanding. It arises from a person realizing how their actions are impacting others We all want to be heroes, we want to change when someone shares their pain and requests us to help, so what if the pain is emanating from our behaviors. However, if someone asks us to change, we treat it as an impending danger and we become closed. We may acknowledge it but we will not want to change. Sharing the pain we are causing makes us sensitive, moves us from a state of knowing to a state of awareness.

TYRANNY OF HABIT

Good and bad habits get into an auto mode. This means that we do not need to put in effort to demonstrate them. Let's say you received feedback and you have become aware of a bad habit and sincerely want to change. Is it easy to make the change? You have to consciously experiment the new behaviors. Otherwise old habits take charge. Even when you try consciously, it would take time before you develop expertise in demonstrating the new behaviors. Until then there could be several fiascos living the new behavior. At every step there is a temptation to roll back to old habits. What can prevent this is to keep consciously practicing the new behavior and to keep reflecting on how it is benefiting us.

HOW DO WE MAKE FEEDBACK INTO A VALUABLE TOOL IN THE ANNUAL APPRAISAL PIT STOP?

Most managers tend to give feedback in terms of specific competencies. They start with a few strengths that the person had demonstrated during the last twelve months and then shift to improvement areas. If this is the way in which you give feedback, you could potentially be derailing your team members' careers. People do not use their strengths and weaknesses in compartments. They use them together. In fact, talent consists of the unique way in which a person uses his strengths and weaknesses to create success. I know of a senior manager who is extremely intelligent, has a sharp tongue and is terribly lazy. He could have achieved a lot more if he was a bit more diplomatic and a lot less lazy. So I can tell him to use his strengths better and address his two weak areas.

I would actually be killing his talent through my feedback, provided he takes my feedback seriously.

His talent is the way he leverages his strengths and so called weak areas. His intelligence coupled with sharp tongue ensures that the quality of discussion is high with his internal customers and consultants that he works with. Being lazy means that there is a lot of space for people to think through and execute. People who work with him enjoy his leadership as they get high quality inputs from him, they push themselves to think better and have complete freedom to think through and execute.

People in general know about their strengths and weaknesses. Feedback is a process of helping people to become aware of their talent by the way they combine their strengths and weaknesses. The reason why people have challenges in using their talent consistently is because they do not mix the strengths-weaknesses potion effectively in the context of a specific situation. Helping people to prepare and execute this talent potion helps make feedback a game changing process.

Once you made the person aware of his talent, focus on feed forward. What does this mean? Essentially it means that you as a manager are not going to be a passive feedback giver to your team member about his past performance behaviors. You truly care about the person and want to see him demonstrate the company competencies and values in full measure. So you want the person to use his strengths effectively and remove any blocks that stunt his talent. **Do you want to try this out?**

LAP 5 – SECTOR IV

DEVELOPMENT PLANNING THROUGH THE APPRAISAL PIT STOP

Development planning through the Appraisal Pit Stop

Do you plan training and development around the strengths of your team member or do you do it around their weaknesses? In general we find that a) appraisal discussions are around the individual's weaknesses and b) most often these weaknesses are addressed through training.

Every employee's individual weakness that needs to be addressed through training is then consolidated into a training calendar. Just imagine an organization consolidating the weaknesses of the entire organization and creating a plan to address those weaknesses. Doesn't this sound absurd? To make it look professional, you have a training head, three smart MBAs to assist the training head, one support staff to put the training needs from the appraisal into an excel document and prepare graphs and half a dozen external trainers to conduct training. A training budget of an organization that has a turnover of 5000 crores and above could be anywhere from 2-10 crores per year.

But if development planning through appraisal pit stops were to be focused on employee strengths, the collective strength of the organization can be enhanced. And weaknesses are best addressed by collaborating with others who hold complementary strengths. After all the purpose of an organization is to collaborate to achieve a goal and that can happen only when weaknesses of one are buttressed by strengths of others. This is elaborated in the section below which examines some of the paradigms in the organization that contribute to ineffective development planning.

Organizational Weakness Management

What happens when you work on your strengths? You enhance them. Similarly what happens when you work on your weaknesses? Ditto. You enhance them.

When you create an organization, you do so based on some core strengths. Then you hire people who can live those strengths through your current and future products, services and solutions. This is how you build a successful enterprise. You do not create an organization as a vehicle to eliminate your core weaknesses. Why would you want to pay people for working on their weaknesses? While this sounds terribly logical and many HR folks reading this would say that they know this anyways, if they honestly reflect on how their training calendars are designed, it would come back to organizational weakness management.

Sounds interesting, you may say. But don't we need to help the person who has weaknesses that are stunting his performance and growth? In the appraisal discussion, in general, managers give feedback on specific competencies and values that the person needs to demonstrate to a greater degree. For example, if a person is weak in planning, the manager would give feedback on the same, give examples and help the person to think through how to plan better. Sounds logical? Yes. However there is a problem here. What if planning is not part of the person's talent? The person is more of a doer. Let's say that the person knows how to get people to execute. This is the talent of the person. Effective feedback should center on how to help this person use his people skills to plan effectively. This would mean how could the person learn how to use another's talent in planning better? Can you see the drift? You are helping the person to use his strengths and talents to address his weaknesses. Do you see that there is a greater chance of success through this approach?

PROUD TO BE A TRAINING OUTFIT

The way many senior managers proudly claim that their organization is a training outfit; they should seriously start a placement wing and make money. These managers attribute the excellent learning opportunities that they provide to their employees as the reason for people getting better opportunities outside. While no one intends to wake up managers living in this fallacy, others need to be aware of the erroneous belief of such claims.

Why am I saying this?

Most training programs are classroom based. Very few companies like Unilever, P&G and GE have strong coaching and career management processes. In fact, while these companies may say that they are talent factories for other companies, they have minimum turnover and lose their second rate people who probably may still qualify as first rate in other companies. Apart from a handful, most companies rely largely on classroom training for development. In a study done by Princeton University, it was found that classroom training has minimal impact - only 10%.

At the same time, most training needs are actually cultural issues. They have to be addressed systemically and not really through training alone. For example, many organizations call me to conduct workshops on performance management because they feel that managers do not give sufficient importance to the development part of the appraisal. They want me to design and conduct performance management workshops. Their ask is, can you help our managers to become better people managers? What they actually mean is that managers respect their team members, listen to them, provide SMART feedback, engage with them regularly and make them successful. But isn't this exactly what managers do with their customers' day in and day out? Aren't these the very same skills that they demonstrate with their bosses and customers? If this is so, why is it that the same managers do not demonstrate these very skills that made them successful with their customers and bosses, with their reportees? This is not an individual issue and this means any development that needs to be brought in has to be at the organizational level.

ASSUMING THAT PULLING THE PERSON OUT OF THE JOB AND GIVING INPUTS WILL SOLVE THE PROBLEM

It is amazing how many team-building workshops happen across the industry. It is supposed to be for bonding, trust building and building a collaborative environment. How come then the employee survey data of many companies and most teams is far from satisfactory? This is simply because you cannot pull out people from work, excite them with some games, derive some leaning and tell them now to apply the same at work. This is not how learning happens. Teamwork discussions have to happen at the workplace. Real issues have to be used to reflect on how we work as a group and what we can do to become a high performance team. Nobody became a Sachin Tendulkar by watching television and eating potato chips. If you want to master the game of cricket, you have to sweat it out on the ground.

Not involving the boss in learning

It is a common sight in companies, wherein the team member comes to his manager for permission to go for a training workshop for he has received an invite from HR. Managers are rarely consulted and they are almost never part of design of development interventions. That is why you find that Managers also do not show enthusiasm for what workshop the team member is going to and what he has learnt after attending the workshop. One reason why bosses are not involved is because it is believed that in a classroom training of 20-30 participants, it is not possible to individualize training.

Training as Recreation

A sure way to get participants into a workshop is choosing the right venue. The address makes the difference. Tired employees want to refresh themselves in the swimming pool. It is also a time to delight your taste buds. It is not unusual for participants to come late for the workshop and then demand that they be let off very early. All these reasons are probably also one of the reasons why training budgets are slashed exactly when people probably need to re-invent themselves. Development budgets are the first casualty of any cost cutting exercise. While one could attribute this to the short-term orientation of management teams, it probably is also because development is seen as a good to do kind of exercise, rather than a game changer for individuals and the organization.

If your organization is a prisoner of incorrect paradigms, you may break the chains by seeking inspiration from some of the development practices given in the next page.

THE ESSENCE OF DEVELOPMENT – INTERESTING PRACTICES

Under each example I have shared my perspective about the pit stop, what organizations can learn and conditions critical to make this practice work for your organization.

Sapient's Career Manager Program: In order to support an individual's career aspirations, Sapient has introduced a Career Manager Program. Each individual in the company is assigned a career manager. This program focuses on an individual's long-term growth through frequent mentoring and developmental inputs provided by the Career Manager.

Rather than taking pride in "weeding out" underperformers Sapient takes pride in their successful performance improvement program that has been able to turn around 70 per cent of underperformers.

Most organizations provide career coaches only to high potential employees. The conventional logic is that career development is relevant only for those who have demonstrated high performance in their current role. These employees are high performers who can now be groomed for higher roles and responsibilities. Hence a career manager or coach makes immense sense. Sapient debunks this thought process and supports every employee with career managers. After all everyone has aspirations. If people think through their aspirations with their Career Manager, they can also reflect about what aspects of their existing talent do they need to enhance. This automatically impacts current performance. This is systemic thinking at it's best. In my opinion Sapient's Career Manager Program is a great development pit stop.

At **American Express** team members are selected as Subject Matter Experts (SME). In this role they continue to be a part of their original functional teams and based on any future ramp-up, they are deputed as Shadow Trainers. In this capacity they are solely responsible for managing the learning curve of the learners assigned to them. They are also required to coach and regularly share feedback. At the end of the rotation the SMEs return to their Team Leader. A certificate of successful completion of the job rotation is awarded.

There is enough research data to support that peer-to-peer learning is the most effective form of learning. This is the most under utilized opportunity in organizations. American Express's development pit stop has another benefit. We learn through imitation. Hence by designating peers as subject matter experts, the organization is directing the attention of fellow peers to the best of what exists in the company.

Godrej Consumer Products has different cross-functional teams, which operate, at different levels. Membership into these teams gives exposure to Senior Management and opportunities to work in strategic or cross-functional initiatives. Notable among them is the Young Executive Board – an initiative intended to energize and motivate young decision makers.

No simulation can ever substitute real experience. One can attend some of the top leadership training programmes at ISB, Harvard and the IIMs. However when it comes to applying the simulated learning in real work situations, it is always different. For sports buffs, it is like learning to bowl well by aiming at a mannequin verses bowling to a real quality batsman. By providing opportunities to work in strategic and cross-functional teams, people get real exposure to business thinking.

One important factor that differentiates leaders from others is the ability to take decisions. Smart risk taking capability helps in decision-making. The Young Executive Board is a wonderful opportunity for high potential individuals in learning to take real business and cross-functional decisions. Over time the organization can also evaluate who among the young leaders have the risk taking capability to grow the organization.

Honeywell Technologies provides employees with tools, which they can use to assess their current competency level and also get it ratified by their supervisors online.

Authentic feedback in itself is an important development tool. You would be surprised to know that most development interventions provide every thing except honest feedback. Hence, most of the time, people go through the process as a good to do activity. Direct stakeholder feedback articulates the 'What's in it for me (WIIFM) for the employee and compels the person to take responsibility for self-development.

Procter & Gamble France, a commercial products group for food service, lodging, commercial cleaning, laundry, vending, office coffee industries and janitorial supply distributors company offers the opportunity for employees to experience another job within the company while taking part in the program "Broadening assignment." As part of this program, employees can hold a new function for a predetermined period of one or two years. At the end of this test period, the employee can decide to stay in this new function or to move back to their previous function.

Exposure of employees to other departments or locations for a week to a month is common practice. While any such exposure has value, it does not provide enough time for a person to gain a deeper appreciation of the department. Working for one to two years actually builds competency and also helps the employees to become clear if the initial interest in the new function was a passing fad or an enduring passion to make a career in the new function or leverage the new function for a career in business management.

Airtel sends its employees on secondment to other Group Companies and on Talent Exchange programs with other affiliate companies. Such secondments and overseas assignments help to develop talents/leadership and improve retention of talent. The duration of assignments could be short or long term i.e. – Short-term assignments (3 - 6 months) – Long-term assignments (> 1 year).

If members work with each other for a considerable time, they start accepting each other for who they are. This means that the team leverages each other's strengths without really getting bogged down by the idiosyncrasies of each member. Members who work in such teams may assume that their irritating qualities do not really matter However these blind spots can actually become career stunting. Hence secondment to group and affiliate companies helps employees to learn how to manage their flip sides better. Over time secondments also help employees to adapt their leadership style to suit different people and situations.

LAP 6
MID YEAR APPRAISAL PIT STOP

Lap 6 – Sector I

Is mid year review a time for hide and seek with your HR function?

How often do the teams that seem to be losing midway actually win the game?

How often do individuals who were behind the leader, surge ahead and win a race?

Is there something that they do in their mid review that triggers midway acceleration?

1972 Munich Olympics. It is the 10,000 m final. LasseViren trips and falls down midway in the race only to get up and win gold in record time.

At the start of the Munich Games, LasseViren, the 23-year-old Finnish policeman from the small village of Myrskyla, was not widely known. Indeed, the heats of the 10,000 meters were his Olympic debut. But when he stumbled and fell just before the halfway mark in the final his chance of victory seemed to have evaporated. The Tunisian Mohamed Gammoudi (who had won the 5,000 meters at the 1968 Olympics) tripped over Viren and gave up two laps later.

But the Finnish runner calmly got to his feet and chased his way back into contention, overtaking Britain's David Bedford, the long-time leader, to not only win the gold medal, but set a world record of 27min 38.4sec. Ten days later, he also won the 5,000m (in an Olympic record time) – a double that he repeated in Montreal in 1976.

When he fell down, something must have triggered in Lasse Viren's mind. The trigger stepped up his performance and eventually contributed to his victory.

It is said that Australian sports teams are more dangerous if they are trailing against their opponents at the midway stage. Similarly, if you observe the middle and long distance races, the athletes who are trailing close to the leader at mid stage seem in general to win the races. Of course this does not apply if the leader has taken a decisive lead.

Hence people who trail at mid stage can actually win you the game.

Can Losing Lead to Winning

Jonah Berger of the Wharton School and Devin Pope of Booth School of Business analyzed more than 18,000 professional basketball games. They concluded that being slightly behind at halftime leads to a discontinuous increase in winning percentage. Teams behind by a point at halftime, for example, actually win more often than teams ahead by one, or approximately six percentage points more often than expected. This psychological effect is roughly half the size of the proverbial home-team advantage. Analysis of more than 45,000 collegiate basketball games finds consistent, though smaller, results. Experiments corroborate the field data and generalize their findings, providing direct causal evidence that being slightly behind, increases effort. These findings illustrate that losing can sometimes lead to winning.

Their analysis focused on halftime for a number of reasons. First, feedback helps people adjust their effort to meet their goals (Locke and Latham 2002), and the break provides a chance for all players to be aware of the score. Second, time to consider one's relative position should invite reflection and increase the salience of the reference point. Third, especially in situations where performance depends on members working together, increased performance is more likely if everyone understands where they stand relative to the goal. Overall, because of the sustained break, halftime provides an ideal opportunity for all team members to know their position relative to their opponent, reflect on it, discuss it, and become motivated.

In organizations, employees do not experience the fall or that trigger until the annual appraisal pit stop. It is just like an athlete getting a shake up from the coach just before the medal distribution ceremony. Such a pity, it is too late. The shake up at the time of medal distribution only creates negative dissatisfaction. A despondent feeling that if only I woke up or someone woke me up when the race was still on.

Given its potential for performance turnaround, It is a wonder that corporates do not take the mid year appraisal pit stop seriously. The paradigm that exists in the mind of several managers is that mid year review is a review of the last six months and is a useless and boring HR process. It is not understood as a mid year accelerator – a process that helps in shifting gears and helping a person trailing in the race midway into a winner.

LAP 6 – SECTOR II

CONVERTING MID YEAR REVIEW INTO A MID YEAR ACCELERATOR

How can we convert our pit stops into mid race game changers?

How do you handle the mid year pit stop of your team members? Do you use or waste the opportunity to convert the mid year review into a mid year accelerator?

A manager can make the mid point of an assignment, project or a goal into a review that can become an accelerator for peak performance. This is irrespective of where his team member is at the mid stage – well ahead, trailing behind or in a hopeless state. Let's explore how this can happen with your team.

Good is the enemy of Great

At the mid stage, some of your team members would be clearly ahead of others. Their attitudes and skills are superior to others. They may have sound execution discipline. Hence you give them the most challenging projects, give them public recognition and advocate their talents in the organization. However, many times such individuals start slipping and sliding back. This happens more often because serial wins at times create a sense of boredom, arrogance and complacency. This is the beginning of the slide downwards. It is so slow that initially it is not observable. Then it catapults like a landslide, catching you totally unaware. How often have we seen athletes lose that critical opportunity to create a world record; how often have we seen the person leading almost till the last lap, end up with no medals.

Challengers have a clear reference point. Winners have no immediate reference points. Actually staying far ahead can become boring over a period of time. It's not at all challenging. Many early winners in corporates jeopardize their winning plot and in the process end up not living up to their full potential. So how do you make such a person stay on course? You shake the person from complacency at the mid stage by giving feedback but not on internal performance benchmarks. You provide feedback on *external performance benchmarks.* You move the reference point from what was internal to the external.

For example, you may tell your high performer:

"You have done extremely well within your team. But ___ members from other teams or other organizations have scored higher than you. Do you want to surpass them?"

"You stand out in the group as the best performer. What goal do you want to set that would challenge you? What behaviors do you want to focus on?"

"You are our top performer. You can help your team to succeed by taking up a higher goal. What goal would you like to take up to make your team a winner?"

When Australia won its first world cup they were already the top ranking team in the world. Steve Waugh set the goal for the team of winning the world cup thrice. When they won the Ashes consecutively, he set the goal of winning the upcoming series in all the continents. When they started winning in all the continents he set the goal of a world record for winning consecutive matches. Over the course of their career as a team, the Australian cricketers surprised themselves by constantly setting a new performance bar.

Once you have helped a high performer agree about a clear reference point and have made the person aware of the gap between where the person is and where the person *could be* – you have created positive restlessness in him/her and the person will take the responsibility of addressing the gap.

USE MID YEAR APPRAISAL FOR SETTING PEOPLE FREE FROM THE 'OK PERFORMANCE' TRAP

Average performers get feedback regularly about the gaps in their performance. Why then, do they not change? This is because over time, such people become used to average performance as an unchangeable reality about them; the negative outcomes of their average performance become a habit. Unfortunately once we acquire a habit, we do not know how to break out of it. Put in another way, any improvement feedback hurts. Makes us uncomfortable for some time. But very soon we become comfortable with the discomfort. So you find little or no change in the patterns of behavior of underperforming employees. In the absence of alternate ideas, we get into the rut of being a perpetual underperformer.

How can we transform an average performer using the mid year appraisal as a mid year accelerator? We can do this by creating positive restlessness but in a manner that is different from the previous category of high performers.

Here the *reference point is internal*. The focus of the feedback should be on the gap between what the person has committed to and what he/she has achieved.

Reflect on the sample feedback given below:

You are slightly behind the top performers in your team. Your potential is much higher than what you achieved. You should expect more from yourself.

If you do better than what you have done till now, you would be not only making yourself successful, but importantly your team can collectively succeed. This will also do justice to your inherent talent. If not, you would not only be failing yourself but also failing the team.

See if your feedback has created positive restlessness in the person- a sense of urgency to immediately do things differently. This is the first step. Do not leave the person here. Ask the person now to reflect on his/her pattern of behaviors in situations where the person did not measure up to expectations. If we look at what works and does not work for us, we see a pattern of behaviors, which help us to succeed or fail. Identifying such scripts and changing the scripts helps a person improve his/her own performance. Let's take an example:

Let's say your team member makes commitments and does not meet them as promised. He never delivers his promise. This seriously erodes his credibility. Nobody trusts his commitments. Let's say you gave him straight feedback and created positive restlessness. Now he genuinely wants to change and wants support. Use this tool now. Ask him to take an instance where he did not meet the commitment.

Share step by step what he thought and did which led to the bad outcome. Put it on paper as the person is sharing step by step. Then ask the person what step he wants to change for a different outcome. Changing the step is changing the script. When he shares what he does step by step, he may realize that he makes commitments without micro planning. He may add micro planning as a step before making the commitment. That will change his outcomes.

Simple isn't it? When your average performers change their scripts, they become super performers.

TAKE THE UNDERPERFORMING EMPLOYEE BY SURPRISE

Imagine you are right now participating in a race where you are way behind. You can see people ahead of you. The spectators are cheering the leaders of the race. There are a few sympathetic spectators trying to cheer you. You are feeling bad right now that they pity you. You wish you could disappear or at least that the spectators lose sense of the direction of the race. Better still, if only your opponents who are far ahead change their priorities. You are not feeling good about yourself and suddenly your coach appears to tell you how terrible he is feeling about your performance, what it is that you are doing wrong and how important it is for you to give your best and not let him down. You hear him out as you have no other choice. Does what he said energize you, bring you back to life and make you give that extra? Not too sure. Now imagine a scenario where the crowds are cheering you saying they know you can do it- you have it in you. Your coach is egging you to do better and saying he trusts your ability to win the race, you have it in you and that you can push yourself because you have the stamina. Would this energize you? Very likely yes.

In the same vein, during the mid year appraisal you need to evoke the underperforming member's pride in a powerful and positive manner. You need to give a strong message that the person's potential is much higher than what the person himself/herself thinks. This is different from just giving a strong message. It is giving tough feedback in the context of potential. This makes the person understand that you trust him/her to do very well. However, this can work only if you genuinely believe in the individual's potential.

Low performers too become comfortable with discomfort. While they get maximum feedback and management attention, they get used to their self-image of a loser. Typically the feedback to them centers on their inadequacies and limitations. Underperformers also take home the message that their poor outcomes are impacting those immediately above and below them, which creates a greater sense of helplessness and paralysis. The more improvement feedback you give to such people, the more it reinforces the image they have about themselves. Hence the traditional improvement feedback route is ineffective with such individuals. Instead of focusing on what he/she has not managed to do, get them to articulate their aspirations; celebrate even minor positive outcomes they may have had. By focusing on people's aspirations and achievements (however minuscule they may be) you are creating a sense that they can change and that they have something valuable to offer to the company. This helps the person to move from an anxiety and apathy mode to one of positive restlessness.

Consider the following example of transformational feedback:

"I want to listen to your aspirations and how you want to realize them. If you are willing to take responsibility for your current performance, I can give you feedback on what would enable you to turn around your performance."

Do you see a difference between the normal feedback we give to low performers and how this feedback has been structured? Here you want to very clearly connect with the person's aspirations. You want to kindle hope (by celebrating the person's aspirations) and do some straight talk. This time around the person is more likely to listen because you demonstrated your commitment to what is most important to the person.

Mid year performance review pit stop is a great time to apply these principles to accelerate the performance of your team members. After all, what is the role of a leader? It is to unlock people's potential. You can do it through creating positive restlessness in that individual and supporting the person's transformation process. If you simply celebrate high performers, keep an eye on under performers and wield the whip on low performers, you are being an immature leader. However, if you want to be a leader of choice, you should be able to decipher the performance code of each of your team members and use positive restlessness in different ways to make people's potential come alive.

WHY MID YEAR? WHY NOT END YEAR?

By mid year, you can observe performance variances. Importantly, there is sufficient time to do course corrections. That way year-end review serves only as a post mortem. In the mid year unlike the end year, reward stakes are absent. Hence it is also good time for the Manager to hold difficult conversations (competencies/ values/ working style).

The added benefit is this. If you can reduce the skew by identifying and plugging in performance leakages in individuals during the mid year reviews, you can build a high performing team. The performance in a normal team when plotted on a graph looks like a normal distribution curve. When you work on individuals and help them to realize their peak, the graph becomes a sharper inverted U.

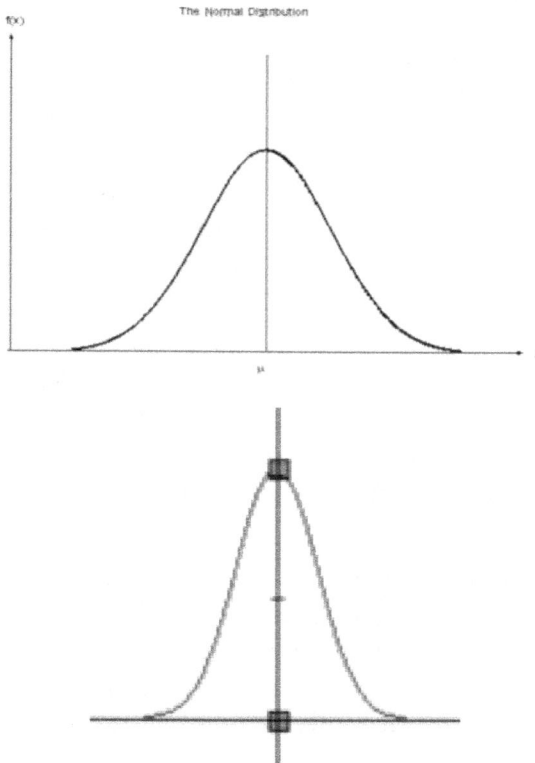

The first graph represents how a normal performance distribution in a team looks. Here the high performers are carrying the load of under performers. This kind of working is unsustainable in the long run. High performers may wonder why they should carry others' load. Somewhere it affects what the team can collectively achieve. Hence when you use the mid review to address the peak performance potential of high performers and under performers, you have activated the dormant potential in each member of the team.

HOW DO YOU MAKE THE MID YEAR REVIEW INTO A MID YEAR ACCELERATOR?

Was there an occasion where as a manager you were working with a team member whose performance was below par? You upped the performance of this team member significantly in a very short period of time and the person never looked back. What did you do which made the significant performance increase happen? What happened to that person as a result of your intervention? You may also look at instances where somebody enabled you to up your performance. What did the person say and do? How did it affect you? What made the change happen? Do not worry if you are not able to think of any examples from work life. Look at examples outside your work life. Maybe in your family?

Do you notice that in each of the cases, your team member already knew that there was a problem though he or she may or may not take responsibility for the same? You helped the person with insights about his or her attitudes and behaviors and how by changing the way they behave, or do things, they can be successful.

Now the question to ask is, do you in any of your monthly/quarterly reviews talk to your team member as a person, about his deeper attitudes and behaviors that impact performance? Are these meetings to transform the person? To change an individual member's mindset? Not really. These meetings are more about the task and how to improve the task and not really about the person behind the task.

Mid Year Reviews do exactly that. A mid year review is about 'who', the person behind the task is, not just about the "Task". Task reviews happen all the time. During mid-year appraisals what we do is a behavioral review. This is not about numbers; it is about behaviors that will make the numbers happen.

If we look around us we will find many examples of such mid reviews.

Let's take a one-day international cricket game. You are the coach of the team. The team is down by 4 wickets and trailing by 200 runs. It is lunchtime. What will you tell the team? Will you tell them "Guys, you are down by 4 wickets and need to make 200 runs? Stay focused and make it happen." Don't they know the score and the wickets that are remaining? Don't they know that they need to make it happen? They know it already. So how will this feedback help? This task feedback will not be of any use.

So what feedback will you give them? The feedback that would really help is on mindset, strategy and technique. You would probably be talking about how to constantly rotate strike, which bowler to pick up to score and whom you should not. When you discuss how to achieve the goal rather than concentrate only on the goal, you achieve a turnaround.

Let's reflect on Parent/Teacher meetings.

How many of you go for Parent/Teacher meetings? When you attend the meeting does the teacher discuss the marks the student – which is your child, has achieved? I don't think so. You anyway get periodic report cards and subject wise test papers. So what does the teacher talk about?

Since you are already aware of how your child is scoring, would knowing the same have any benefit to you? What would be of greater use for you? Marks or behaviors that have resulted in those marks? Would it make sense to you if the teacher spends significant time on the positive and performance stunting behaviors? The teacher probably would share with you about your child's attention span that needs improvement, the need for your child to practice regularly, that your child has extraordinary musical talent that could be channelized better. This is what enables you to work on your child to improve him/her.

Is there learning for us from Sports and Parent Teacher meetings? So, if for success in these arenas, review is important, how can corporate environment be any different? Mid-Reviews, unknowingly, is part of our lives – personal as well as professional. But, the question is, are we capitalizing on these? Or do we waste time by focusing on the task feedback without going into the behaviors that govern the task. Do we in the name of feedback share what the team member already knows – numbers that indicate that (s)he has done well or not. Is there an opportunity for us to leverage behavioral feedback a lot more than what we are doing right now?

If you want your team members to succeed – and in their success lies your success – isn't it imperative for you to share how to improve as much as what to improve? Is it not important to hold mid-reviews as an integral part to enable their success?\

Triggering positive restlessness for mid year acceleration

When your manager gave you feedback to step up your performance, what happened to you immediately after you received the feedback? Did it make you feel uneasy? Did it give rise to discomfort? Did it have an impact on what you did after this? After the feedback did you back to work with more hunger, with a deep commitment to do better, to win for yourself and the team? Did you become more focused? If your answer is yes, it shows that the feedback that you received from your colleague impacted your heart and the mind and made you perform at a greater level of excellence. It created a pressure on you to perform – which translated to focus better. It means that this feedback created positive restlessness in you.

When you give feedback to a person that makes him/ her demand more from oneself, you have created positive restlessness in that person. You may say is this not equivalent to creating anxiety, some stress and a bit of panic? In fact it is exactly the opposite. Anxiety stunts performance. Positive restlessness motivates a person for higher performance. For example, when you say, "I am not happy with your performance," you create anxiety in the person. However, when you genuinely say, "Given the kind of potential you have, I am disappointed with your performance" you create positive restlessness. Mid Year Review in essence is a performance accelerator. It creates the positive restlessness to bounce back and succeed. If someone is already doing very well, a new reference point creates positive restlessness to set sights on greater heights.

Feedback that creates positive restlessness

Someone who is the top performer in the team	Someone whose performance is below par	Someone who has delivered low performance
"You have done extremely well within your team. But ___members from other teams or other organizations have scored higher than you. Do you want to surpass them?"	"You are behind the top performance expected by the company. Your potential is much higher than what you achieved. You should expect more from yourself."	"I want to listen to your aspirations and how you want to realize them. If you are willing to take responsibility for your current low performance, I can give you feedback on what would enable you to turn around your performance and move towards realizing your aspirations."
"You stand out in the group as the best performer. What goal do you want to set that would challenge you? What behaviors do you want to focus on?"	"If you do better than what you have done till now, you would be not only making yourself successful but importantly your team can collectively succeed. This will also do justice to your inherent talent. If not, you would not only be failing yourself but also failing the team."	

"You are our top performer. You can help your team to succeed by taking up a higher goal? What goal would you like to take up to make your team a winner"		

EARNING THE RIGHT TO MANAGE OTHERS

Once you have given feedback and created positive restlessness to change, it is time to support the person to excel. Without providing support, you have not earned the right to be a manager or a leader. How you could support your team member to accelerate is the focus of the next section.

LAP 6 – SECTOR III

TOOLS YOU COULD USE IN THE MID YEAR PIT STOP FOR ACCELERATING PERFORMANCE

Tools to convert mid year review pit stop into a mid year accelerator

Tool for Giving Straight Feedback

a) Tell the truth because you care. Give behavioral feedback.

You accelerate performance when you talk straight from the heart. Tell your team member what you truly appreciate and where the performance gaps are. Go beyond the numbers. Get into behavioral feedback on each goal.

Examples

1. "The report you created yesterday was well-written, understandable, and made your points about the budget very effectively."

2. "At this morning's meeting I noticed you used all of the allotted time to present your ideas, and didn't allow time for anyone else to share other ideas. Everyone had spent time coming up with ideas and I felt disappointed because we didn't get to hear perspectives of others and might have lost out on valuable ideas. Because they weren't asked to contribute, their expressions showed that they thought the meeting was a waste of time."

Tools for creating Positive Restlessness

a) Shift focus from activities to impact

If a person is excited about the amount of work done, appreciate the person on the effort put in and ask the person about the impact that the effort has led to.

Examples

1. You conducted a great training programme. Participants have given excellent ratings. Do you know the extent to which participants were actually able to use the learning in

the workplace? What has been the impact of the learning on work performance?

2. You introduced kaizen to generate ideas for workplace productivity. In the last five months your efforts have led to five kaizens per person per month. This is commendable. To what extent have these contributions impacted workplace productivity?

b) *Refer to the best that the person did in the past*

Reminding the person the best of what he/she has done in the past makes a person realize the gap between what the person is doing right now and what the person is actually capable of doing.

Examples

1. When you were managing the Lucknow branch, you had enormous pressure and were being pulled in several directions. The way you prioritized your goals, did micro planning, built team capabilities, motivated the team to focus and deliver at high level of excellence made you the best branch head of that year. What can you learn from that experience that you want to use here to replicate such success?

2. The way you presented in front of the senior leadership team was excellent. You were precise to the point, gave clear logic, emphasized the outcomes and gave answers to their queries that clearly addressed their concerns. You were at your best in this presentation. How can you consistently bring out the best when you deliver presentations?

c) *Share relative performance*

When we give higher performance benchmarks we create a sense of urgency in a person.

Examples

1. While we improved on our performance from the last quarter we are behind the actual performance that we delivered in this quarter during the last year.

2. Your production numbers are commendable. However, in relation to the cost you incurred to produce each container there are other production managers who have done significantly better.

3. You are the best performer in your team. Do you want to set your sights higher? The best performers in other zones are ahead of you on sales growth. Do you want to reflect on how you want to step up your performance?

d) Performance vs Aspirations

When we compare the current performance with the aspirations of the individual it creates fire in the belly.

Examples

1. Your aspiration is to be a Manager. An effective manager has to be skilled in building teams. I see you working individually and not by collaborating with others. I was wondering if your current approach will help you to realize your aspirations?

2. Your aspiration is fast track growth. I do not see you investing your time in your learning and development to make this happen.

TOOLS FOR PROVIDING SUPPORT

Once we have given straight feedback and created positive restlessness, it is time to provide continuous support. There are simple ways of providing support. These simple techniques do not eat into your time, do not demand resources and are sure shot winners.

a) *Mirror behaviors*

Provide here and now feedback whenever the person demonstrates the right behaviors and also when the person deviates from his own behavioral commitments.

Examples

1. I saw you appreciate your team member when he showed initiative to take more responsibility.

2. You spoke most of the time in your team meeting.

   (Here you are just mirroring. You are not inferring.)

b) *Connect your team member with role models*

Seeing people demonstrate the right behaviors and actions increases our own conviction about what will work. Ask the person to observe people for specific role model behaviors and also create coaching relations.

Examples

1. Ramesh is great at engaging his team members. It will help if you learn from him what he does to create such high engagement levels.

2. Have you seen how Swathi conducts difficult conversations with our management committee and gets time, money and people support for her initiatives? Watch her approach, and style of convincing others, consciously. See what behaviors you can experiment henceforth.

c) *Change the Script*

If we look at what works and does not work for us, we see a pattern of behaviors, which help us to succeed or fail. Identifying such scripts and changing the scripts helps a person improve their own performance.

Examples

1. Let's say your team member has issues with his internal customer and frequently complains to you.

   "Ravi always puts pressure on me and makes it difficult for me to give my best."

   Ask your team member to change this language to:

   "What can I do to remove Ravi's pressure so that I can make it easy to give my best?"

   In his case will changing the question change the way we think? To a large extent, Yes.

2. Your team member jumps into action before planning. He does not ask questions and get into details. He seems to do all the thinking while doing. Because of this reason his output is sub-par. Ask him to take an instance where he did not meet the commitment. Share step by step what he thought and did which led to the bad outcome. Put it on paper as the person is sharing step by step. Then ask the person what step he wants to change for a different outcome. Changing the step is changing the script. When he shares step by step what he does, he may realize that he makes commitments without micro planning. He may add micro planning as a step before making the commitment. Ask him to experiment these new steps for a few weeks. Be his mirror.

LAP 7
SELF PIT STOP

LAP 7 – SECTOR I
HELLO ME, WAKE UP. THIS IS MY CAREER

When was the last time you really paused and asked

*Am I accumulating several years of the same experience or
Am I really growing?*

How smart are your Self Pit Stops?

Maybe your boss is incompetent and HR is hopeless and only if your organization or your boss or HR changes its way of working, is there any future for you. If you are really lucky, this may just happen - one of these three may change and your wishes may come true. Or if you are really unlucky, it may not happen in your lifetime. The world is rapidly moving towards self-career management. Your organization is interested and is bothered about only its top 10-20% talent. To be fair to the organization, when the company is not certain about its own future, how can the organization craft the future for its entire talent force? If you are part of this 10-20%, be happy. But don't feel too happy either. It takes just a small change in the environment or company strategy for your talent to become less relevant and less important than before and you may slip into oblivion.

If the organization is not managing your talent, have you taken charge of your talent and career? Annual performance reviews, mid year performance reviews, team reviews and one to one periodic reviews that bosses conduct are great opportunities for you to shape your career. It is not as if bosses are conducting these pit stops for you to succeed. However, if you choose so, you can convert these into effective pit stops. If you want to make these into effective pit stops you should first create a positive bias in the mind of your boss and other key stakeholders.

Do you create a positive bias in the people who matter?

Source: www.moillusions.com

Just look at this picture and tell me how many strands of hair this old man has? 3 or 5 or 7? Whatever your answer is, you are almost right. This is a polite way of saying that you are dead wrong. Tell me honestly did you see the warriors on the horse in this picture. You may not have, as I conditioned you to look at the old man and his strands of hair. We are all conditioned by our past experiences. They create our biases. This is so natural that we cannot avoid it. Of course, we can be conscious and deliberately ensure that it does not affect us. The point is conditioning and biases are a way in which we simplify the messy world. Your boss also is a prisoner of biases. He will have a bias about you. If there is no way to escape, why not take advantage of the same? Why not create a positive bias in your boss? When your boss has a positive bias about you, he/she is exploring how to make you successful. So he/she starts asking the right questions to himself/herself and to you.

How can you create a positive bias?

First Things First - Do Not Ask Often About What You Need to Improve

Are you somebody who is looking to improve oneself all the time? So do you always keep asking your boss what you can do better? If yes, you are asking the most stupid question in the world. You can never become successful by working on your weak areas. In fact, no company employs you for your weaknesses and for you to work and improve on those weaknesses. After all your company is not a training center.

Instead ask your boss what he considers as your talent. What are you doing well? How well are you using your strengths? What can you do to strengthen your strengths? The more questions you ask your boss on what is good about you, you are directing his/her attention towards the best of who you are. This will also make him/her think of how to utilize your talents better rather constantly looking into giving feedback on your performance gaps.

Talk of outcomes not efforts

Nobody cares about your efforts. If you take your efforts too seriously you only will feel bad and get emotionally affected by it. Even when you have not achieved results, use the language of outcomes.

Let's say you have not been able to sell a product – When you speak to your boss, the efforts language will read something like this:

"I met several customers today. I went to each one of them with a clear value proposition. I listened to them intently and gave them ideas on how our product would work effectively. While I thought they were convinced about the value of the product, they did not buy the same."

Now let's see how outcome language would sound:

"I am pursuing our strategy of providing solutions and not just selling products. While they seem to be convinced about our value proposition, they are taking time to make a decision. I am wondering how to get a breakthrough."

While your outlook may be the same, your boss is likely to see you as someone who is pursuing the company strategy when you use the outcome language. This apart, using the outcome lenses will help you approach your work differently. Actually, the more you use the outcome language the more you are likely to think through new ideas and new approaches to get the sales breakthrough. If you use the efforts language, you will continue to work harder on the same process even if it is not working.

Once you have managed to create a positive bias in your boss's mind, it is time to make the best use of the planned pit stops that are part of your organizational processes.

APPROACHING THE ANNUAL APPRAISAL PIT STOP

Many people carry wrong notions about their own annual appraisal. It makes life difficult for them and their managers. These notions are as follows:

1. An appraisal is basically a rating exercise

2. Normalization and Relative rating are evil

3. If I am rated as 'Met expectations,' I have not done well

4. If I keep getting far exceed expectations year on year it means that I am doing very well

NOTION 1: APPRAISAL IS BASICALLY A RATING EXERCISE

If you have this notion, you are very likely to treat the appraisal discussion as a war – you have to fight to win. There would be haggling about whether a KRA achievement deserves a 4 or a 3.5. You will not give up. For every example that your appraiser gives about what you could have done better, you will give three examples of where you actually did well, and how the way the appraiser interpreted your role and competencies in the example that the appraiser gave, is incorrect. There is tension all around. In this environment honest conversations cannot happen. It becomes a give and take exercise - a useless pit stop from my perspective.

Appraisal is a year-end comment of the organization about how you have performed on the key goals. This is a crucial feedback session before you embark on the next year. This conversation should help you become aware of your strengths and weaknesses and how you could approach your role and key goals differently in the coming year. Quantitative ratings even when done with the best methodology and intention are misleading. What you need for your success is authentic qualitative feedback. It cannot come unless you demonstrate openness and give permission to your boss not to hold back. When you do that, you are increasing your value as your increased awareness will fetch you better returns from your key goals in the coming years. This does not mean that you should just accept whatever your boss says. If you do not agree to your boss, ask him/her questions to clarify your understanding and in many cases help your boss to become aware of his/her unfair bias. For example, if your boss says that a goal warrants below expectations where as you feel that it should be rated as met expectations ask your boss "What could I have done differently which would have qualified for a met expectation rating? Similarly, on the same, what should I have done to get an exceed expectation rating? By asking questions and making your boss speak, you gain deeper understanding of what you need to do differently. Importantly if you have a point, it will make him/her accountable.

Notion 2: Normalization and Relative ratings
are evil

After all, you have always heard your boss blame the change in your rating to the evil mechanisms of HR or top management. Normalization is a word hated by millions as they consider it unfair. How can people across departments and locations be compared with each other? How can our individual performance be so blatantly undermined?

NORMALIZATION INDICATES CORRECTION

You are basically correcting the biases of bosses who may over rate or under rate in the context of the business and department performances. Haven't you encountered bosses who want to make every team member happy and hence rate everyone as exceeding expectation? Similarly, haven't you met bosses who are not happy with any performance? God forbid, if the team member does manage to exceed expectations he/she is likely to blame it on the weather. So performance actually does not belong to you. Normalization is a means to correct such aberrations, which are more of a rule than an exception in organizations.

If a manager is honest in the way the goals are defined (alignment with the organizational goals, measures of performance and standards expected) and is equally honest in the way the person rated the goal (considering the impact of the goal on department/ organizational goals), there would be no need for normalization.

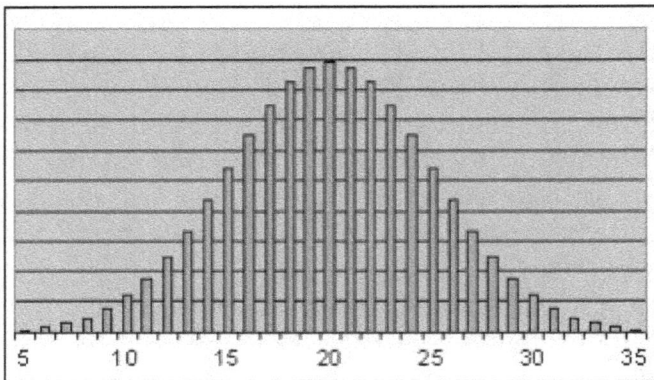

If a department has met expectation performance, this is how the normal distribution of performance of members would look. If the distribution is skewed towards the left and the department/organization has actually done well, it means that the manager was unreasonably tough in rating his/her team members. Instead if the distribution is skewed towards the right and the department/organization has actually not done well, it means that the manager was unreasonably lenient in rating his/ her team members.

A manager has to be honest in his ratings. You can do your bit to help him do so. Focus on what will enhance your value in the long run. It is not ratings. It is your increased awareness of your talent, strengths and showstopper weaknesses. Give your boss the permission to be honest. However, do not let a scheming manager get away with unfair ratings. Ask questions without getting emotional. Unfair Managers are scared of team members who ask smart questions and make the manager speak.

WHAT ABOUT RELATIVE RATINGS?

Imagine you are the owner of the organization where you are working right now. As an owner, what is it about performance that would bother you? Is it about which departments did well and who within those departments achieved the functional goals? I don't think. You would not care much about functional goals. What would really bother you is whether organizational goals are being met and who contributed the most to realizing them. While support departments often feel that they should not be compared with line functions like sales and operations, if they are truly support functions, they should be able to showcase how their presence accelerated the business rhythm of the line functions. If they cannot showcase their contribution you might feel they have played no role. Hence, if you are the owner you would want to know who among your people made big contributions to the organizational goal and reward them disproportionately. Hence for an owner, differentiation based on relative contribution to outcomes is critical.

You may feel – maybe differentiation based on relative contribution makes sense for an owner, but does not appear fair if I am an employee. I have done what was within my control. How can I be made accountable for something that was some one else's responsibility? That person or that department does not even report to my boss or me. Relative rating is unfair.

PERFECT LOGIC

Just that the assumption that formed the basis of the logic is flawed. You are not paid in an organization to do your work. You are paid to influence outcomes. The biggest influencing is with respect to the customer. It begins from there. If customers have to be influenced, you have to influence your internal customers. If you do not have influencing skills, organizational working is not for you. Influencing is a bread and butter skill along with collaborating. If you do not have these skills and still have a job, someone is doing you a big favor.

Let me ask you a different question. If you were a parent, would you join your child in a school where your child is the best of the lot or would you join your child in a school where there are several comparable students? You probably would opt for the second choice. After all, your child will stagnate if there is no comparable excellence. Relative ratings help you to know where you stand. It gives you a yardstick to measure your own level of excellence and continuously improve. Without relative rating you are a frog in the well.

RELATIVE RATINGS PROMOTE EXCELLENCE

When you go to a grocery store for any purchase, do you expect to be provided with alternative options for every product that you want to buy? If yes, why is it important to you to have choices? Maybe, because you can choose the one that serves your need best. As a customer, your belief may also be that competition between different companies will ensure quality and keep the cost down.

Let's take this analogy into our organizational setting. Each person in your team is a monopoly. You do not keep two people for doing the same work. Even if you do it for some positions, in general that is not how organizations work. Take for instance your own self. You probably are a CEO or a VP of a function or a Head of a Region or a Manager of a department or a section or an executive in a particular area. You are the only person handling the role that has been assigned to you. The role is crucial for organizational success. However, even if you are performing below par, at least until the organization keeps you on their payroll they have to bear with your mediocrity. If the organization is full of monopolist role holders, how can you still get the best out of each of them? That is possible if we create a common performance yardstick.

While you have several team members performing different roles, what you expect from them is the same – contribution to organization goal – top line (revenues) or the bottom line (profitability) or the new line (realized opportunities in new areas). Hence, when you compare these individual monopolists using a 'contribution to business' yardstick, you promote excellence.

Notion 3: If I have been rated as 'Met Expectations' I have not done well

Goals or Key result areas are challenging, have stretch and are interconnected with goals of other individuals and departments. Hence if every one meets their goal expectations, the organization will become a high performance organization. Hence if you met expectations on any of the goals pat yourself. You have done well.

In fact exceeding expectations in some situations can be detrimental to the organization. Let's say 20% of the employees of your organization received a rating of exceeds expectations. This could mean that these 20% have taken the load of those who were under performing and hence have made significant contribution to the organization. This is great.

However, if their 'exceed expectations' achievement caught the organization unawares, the fabulous performance may actually become a huge liability for the organization. Imagine a sales manager who commits 100 crore sales and brings in 150 crore sales. He has over exceeded performance expectations.

However, the operations may not have been prepared to handle this additional sale. Pulling out the rabbit from the pocket looks good in a circus, but in organizational life doing such clownish acts puts the organization under tremendous pressure in the short run and loose its reputation in the long run. Hence exceed and far exceed can actually undermine an organization. Do not aim for setting lower targets and over achieving them. If you do so, you are just playing a game. A game wherein your organization is encouraging self goals.

NOTION 4: IF I KEEP GETTING FAR EXCEED EXPECTATIONS YEAR ON YEAR IT MEANS THAT I AM DOING VERY WELL

Let's say you take up a new role that is sufficiently challenging and has tremendous scope for you to learn. Can you in the same year that you have taken up the new responsibility get exceed expectations? If you met expectations that year you should consider yourself as having done very well. The next year your performance in that role will become better and the year after, even better. So in any role you go through a process of continuous improvement, which is reflected in shift from one level on the rating scale to another.

Look at the ratings that you have been getting. If you are always exceed expectations or more, it actually means that your role has not changed for a long time and actually you are stagnating professionally. It may be good for your boss and your organization to keep you there as you are supposedly indispensible. However, it is disastrous for you to be in that comfort zone for long.

So be concerned about your career if every year you get a far exceeds expectation rating.

Do you look at your performance year on year?

Or

Do you see it as something that is spread across years?

If you notions are in the right place, it is time for you to make the best use of annual appraisals as a pit stop. Self reflect on how you generally approach the annual appraisal pit stop. Given below are statements that reflect an orientation towards the annual appraisal. Tick what is largely applicable to you.

My Annual Appraisal Pit Stop	Tick
I do not collect evidence for my performance appraisal meeting because I assume that my boss knows what I've done.	
I assume that because my boss gave me no feedback, it means that I must be doing well.	
The primary objective of the appraisal meeting is to influence my boss to get a high rating.	
My manager's feedback during the appraisal generally surprises me.	
High effort = high performance.	
The benchmark for evaluating my performance should be my individual output only.	
I assume my appraiser knows how important the appraisal is for me.	
My development is primarily the responsibility of my manager and HR. I merely do what I am told.	

Reflect on your rating. Decide what you intend to change. After all, you are the master of your own destiny.

Lap 7 – Sector II
What if your appraiser is a Bad Manager?

Let's say your appraiser is a bad manager - the kind who does not care about giving honest feedback, is not supportive and importantly does not set aside time for appraisal discussions. He/she may not even come prepared. Are you going to hand over the fate of the appraisal pit stop to this person? Or are you going to channelize the conversation so that it helps you in your personal and professional growth and high performance?

If you agree to take charge, what questions are you going to ask?

Indicative questions for appraisee	
Question	Rationale
How did I perform? Can you give me specific incidences so that it can help me in my own development?	Many appraisers feel uncomfortable giving feedback in difficult situations. By asking for feedback you are giving explicit permission to the appraiser to give honest feedback.
(Contextual- Appraiser's outlook is that of a glass half empty) Can you give me feedback on what I did well? What are my core strengths?	You are inviting the appraiser to look at what he/she values most about what you do, makes the appraiser look at the glass half full.
Can you advise me on how I should approach my improvement areas? What support can I expect from you to overcome my weaknesses?	You share responsibility for your development plan with your appraiser and seek support beyond classroom training – like coaching, mentoring, networking etc.
I would like to ask the following two things: Which projects and teams can I look forward to being a part of? What is your aspiration for me?	Helps you understand what the appraiser thinks about your future in the organization.

(Context - The appraiser disagrees with feedback that the appraiser has given) What could I have done differently which would have classified me as Met Expectations/ Exceed Expectations/ Far Exceed Expectations?	Helps you gain a perspective on how you could have performed better as per the appraiser.

HOW CAN YOU STRENGTHEN YOUR ANNUAL APPRAISAL PIT STOP?

How regularly do you seek feedback from your internal and external customers on how well YOU are serving them? What are they excited about your service and what would they like you to change?

In general each one of us serve four different people.

Those who use your services They do not understand the technicalities of what you do. However, they can give you feedback on whether your services are adding value to their work or not. They generally give feedback on timeliness, ease of use and relevance.

Those who can appreciate the technical quality of your work These people know as much as you know, probably more. They are your bosses, peers and in some cases people with similar background like you who work with your client. They critique your approach, methodology and process. They generally give feedback on the reliability and validity of your design and methods. They give the stamp of credibility to your technical competence.

Those who understand the return on investment (ROI) from the current and future perspective Your business heads are interested only in how your work is impacting the business outcomes. Is it contributing to the top line or the bottom line? Is it strengthening the core competencies? Is it making the processes agile and adding value to the customer, your internal customers and the company? They want to know your business value and how much effort you have put in, or how right you are about your approach.

Those who are guided by you These are your team members. They look up to you for direction and motivation. Is your leadership style helping them to become capable and valuable? Are you creating an environment that makes them come to work every day and give in their best? These are the questions that are important to them.

If you want to have a great annual appraisal discussion, seeking feedback from these key stakeholders regularly is very important. The feedback helps you to stay focused. More importantly, your stakeholders see your intent and reach out to make you successful.

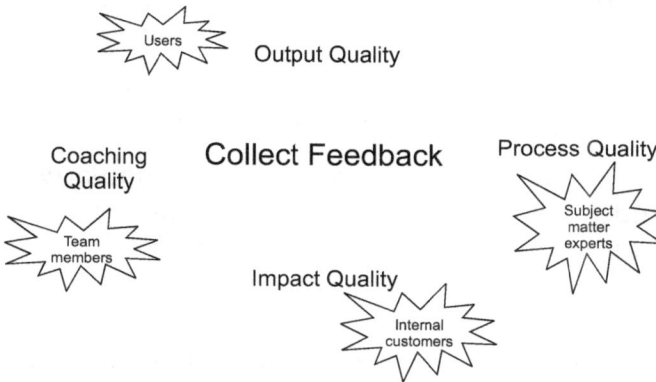

Once you have collected feedback on your achievements from various sources, how do you present your achievements?

Do you want to write your achievements in such a way that it creates a positive bias?

Consider the four options. Which one would create a positive bias and why?

1. I exceeded the sales target by 120%.

2. I increased the dealer network and exceeded the sales target by 120%.

3. I invested significant time in improving our service quality and built credibility with our existing dealers. They introduced us with strong referrals to competitor dealers in the four geographies where our presence was negligible. My actions resulted in an increase in the dealer network and I exceeded the sales target by 120%.

4. Getting a footstep in the four new geographies was a challenging task because of the dominant presence of our competitors. Together they controlled the entire dealer network. I invested significant time in improving our service quality and built credibility with our existing dealers. They introduced us with strong referrals to competitor dealers in the four geographies where our presence was negligible. My actions resulted in an increase in the dealer network, and I exceeded the sales target by 120%.

Which of the four options constitutes the way you present your achievements in your appraisal pit stop?

I hope you have chosen option 4. This is popularly called the STAR model. It is recommended for resume writing. You can also use it for showcasing your achievements.

For each KRA

Situation   What was the challenge posed by the situation?

Task   What was I expected to achieve?

Actions   What did I do?

Result   What was the impact?

IDEAS TO NEGOTIATE WITH AN APPRAISER WHO IS NOT INTERESTED IN THE ANNUAL APPRAISAL PIT STOP

I share below some ideas on how to communicate with different kinds of appraisers. They are scripts you might want to try out. Even if you don't, think about what the script is intending to convey.

SYMPTOM 1: APPRAISER SEEMS TO BE FRIVOLOUS OR CASUAL ABOUT ANNUAL APPRAISAL

"I know you are busy and have several commitments. However, this discussion is very important to me. I have done some exciting work and I want to take you through my achievements. Similarly, I faced challenges in achieving certain goals. When I reflected on the challenges I was also able to identify my development areas. Sharing all this is going to take time, and I need your attention. If you cannot spend time now, I am open to rescheduling this meeting."

SYMPTOM 2: APPRAISER IS FOCUSING ONLY ON WHAT HAS NOT GONE WELL

"You probably want me to excel and hence are concentrating on improvement feedback. However, what would work well for me is if you share what went well along with what I could have done better. Otherwise, I would assume that I did not add any value through the year."

1. Acknowledge and appreciate the intention
2. Share what approach would help you better

SYMPTOM 3: APPRAISER IS ONLY SPEAKING IN GENERIC TERMS

"I sincerely thank you for appreciating me. I want to take you through each goal using the STAR (Situation-Task-Action-Results) framework that I learnt in a book that I read recently. This will give you the context in which I worked on the goal, what I did and the impact that I was able to create. I sought feedback from my key internal customers on the impact. I want to bring that data also here."

Symptom 4: Appraiser Feedback is Vague

"Thank you for the feedback. I want to work on this area. Can you share what specific behaviors that I need to change? Can you please help me become clear on how this behavior impacted work effectiveness?"

B = Behavior. **Can you please help me understand the specific behavior you observed?**

I = Impact. **Please help me understand the impact of those behaviors on my work effectiveness.**

Symptom 5: Appraiser's rating is not acceptable

"I was expecting 'Met Expectations' on this goal. Can you help me understand what I should have done to get a Met expectation rating?"

When you use questions to understand the feedback better, it is called the Socratic method of dialoguing. Socrates was an extraordinary Greek philosopher. He would ask basic questions and make people realize the faulty nature of their logic. If your appraiser says that your performance was reasonable, instead of arguing that your performance is good, just ask, "Can you please help me understand what makes you feel that my performance is reasonable?" This will make the appraiser become alert and give evidence-based feedback.

What will you do if your boss gives you a high rating that you do not deserve?

Is it possible that your boss does not want to confront you on your performance, just wants to retain you and hence gives you a higher rating that you know you do not deserve? What will you do if this happens to you?

I want to share two examples to help you think through what is a smart approach to handling this situation.

In the 2003 World Cup semi-final against Sri Lanka, Gilchrist was batting well, when a ball from Aravinda De Silva touched his pad-bat and went into the air and was caught by the wicketkeeper. The umpire ruled Gilchrist as not out as he felt the ball hit the pads.

Let's say you are in the place of Gilchrist. You knew that the ball hit your bat as well. However, the umpire has given a not out decision. What would you do? After all you are the batsman, not the umpire. If the umpire gave a not out decision, it is not your fault. That apart, this is a crucial match. You got lucky this time. Take advantage and make the most.

Gilchrist Walked He declared himself out, as he knew that he was out. He set his own standards. He was not willing to live with the lifeline of a poor umpiring decision.

Take another situation.

You see a chick struggling to come out of the eggshell. You can feel the pain and you want to help. You break the shell and help the chick to come out. You feel good about yourself. Great facilitation.

Unfortunately the chick will not survive for too long. What you thought as a noble act would not let it strengthen its wings. With weak wings it cannot protect itself. It would just be a matter of time before it dies.

We are the products of our choices. Please decide your course.

Dishonest winner vs Honest loser.

Winning in the short run vs Winning in the long term.

Lap 7 – Sector III

If the only thing you do not have time for is a development pit stop

Do you face the challenge of not finding time for your own development? Even when you nominate yourself for a training workshop or a cross-functional project, do you withdraw at the last minute? If you do so, you are not alone. Most managers are selfless when it comes to their own development. They sacrifice their own development for the sake of fire fighting and routine management. After a while when they become obsolescent and are asked to go, they wonder what had gone wrong. Many never realize that they compromised their own growth because they cared to get a few brownie points from their bosses by handling the fires and routine well.

Taking charge of one's own development is not complicated. We want to share with you simple ideas that you may like to experiment.

FOLLOW THE 40-60 RULE

At any point of time 40% of what you do should be new to you. Only that would make your job exciting. Every day would then be an adventure. Otherwise you quickly slip into your comfort zone. Your manager may say "Have a heart, how can I get you 40% new work every year? Once in 3-5 years, I will ensure that you get a new role." Do not buy this logic. Your manager can do a lot of things to ensure that your work has 40% new content. For example, he can shuffle work, shuffle part work, nominate you into project teams, second you to another department, and reinvent the department purpose so on and so on. If your manager shows his helplessness, just move out. There is no point working under idiots.

DEVELOP YOUR HOBBY INTO YOUR TALENT

Most of the jobs that we do are either not so interesting or not so important for the organization. It is just that someone senior is too lazy to do our work or the organization is too lazy to dispose of us. Even if the job is exciting, most of us are after all in the red ocean. This means we do work which others can also do. This means there is competition. How about developing something where there is no competition?

When you reflect about your learning and development needs, why not consider sharpening your hobby into a talent. You may or may not want to monetize the same. However, once it becomes a talent, you have more career options.

For example, if you enjoy drawing pictures on your notepad and find it a productive way to keep yourself occupied in a meeting, why not develop your talent in that area. Most notepads are bland and boring. Your drawings can bring energy into notepads and maybe also stimulate ideas in the mind of the person using the notepad. While drawing in meetings is a non-value adding activity, it can make you a millionaire if you develop this hobby into talent.

LAP 8
PAUSE BEFORE THE FINISH

LAP 8 – SECTOR I

THE EFFECTIVE PIT STOP SOLUTION TOOLS AND METHODS

Start by Changing your Lenses

We find that leaders across organizations and industries find it difficult to nurture effective pit stops. The basic reason for this is their wrong notion about what their primary role is. When you ask leaders and managers what their primary role is they define it as achieving high performance. Even if they do not say it in so many words, their performance metrics say it all. For example, the sales heads are accountable for sales numbers; the operations heads are questioned on production and productivity numbers, the CEO is measured on the top line and bottom line. The reality is each of these measures is an outcome. You achieve these as a result of doing something else. As most leaders and managers do not know what this 'doing something else' means, they conveniently become review managers for others. Their time is spent in meetings reviewing others as their own performance is an aggregation of what others achieve.

Unless leaders and managers redefine their primary role, effective pit stops will be an elusive dream.

Their primary role is that of building performance capacities of the organization, teams and individuals. Unless we quiz leaders and managers on what they have done to build organizational, team and individual capacities and how much personal investment of time they have made on capacity building, we will not see a fundamental shift in their role. Any leader/manager's job is to help the individual contributors to become capable high performers. If a Manager has managers reporting to him, his job is to make the managers capable. This is because most managers neither serve customers directly nor produce products/services all by themselves. Hence they cannot be accountable for chasing high performance. They should be accountable for building the capacity in the individuals and teams to achieve high performance. Therefore, an effective solution to promoting pit stops is to debunk leaders and managers who take pride in taking decisions and not in building decision-making capabilities in others.

BECOME AN ACTIVE OBSERVER

If you want to embrace the role of a capability builder, you would need to invest a lot of time in observing, reflecting and gaining insights – about your organization, your customers, your competitors, your team and each individual within (including yourself). When you are leading from the front and are totally immersed in task excellence, you may not really have time to reflect. If you do not reflect enough, you really cannot make the right decisions and course corrections. When you are surprised by a customer feedback survey or employee satisfaction report or by the resignation of an employee or a change in market trends, you know that you have not invested enough in reflection at the right time. If you had done so, you could have dealt with problems as well as leveraged opportunities.

In the article 'Ferguson's Formula' written by Anita Elberse with Sir Alex Ferguson, the legendary coach explains his transition to active observation as the secret of his leadership success.

"When I started as a coach, I relied on several basics: that I could play the game well that I understood the technical skills needed to succeed at the highest level, that I could coach players, and that I had the ability to make decisions. One afternoon at Aberdeen I had a conversation with my assistant manager while we were having a cup of tea. He said, "I don't know why you brought me here." I said, "What are you talking about?" and he replied, "I don't do anything. I work with the youth team, but I'm here to assist you with the training and with picking the team. That's the assistant manager's job." And another coach said, "I think he's right, boss," and pointed out that I could benefit from not always having to lead the training. At first I said, "No, no, no," but I thought it over for a few days and then said, "I'll give it a try. No promises." Deep down I knew he was right. So I delegated the training to him, and it was the best thing I ever did.

"It didn't take away my control. My presence and ability to supervise were always there, and what you can pick up by watching is incredibly valuable. Once I stepped out of the bubble, I became more aware of a range of details, and my performance level jumped. Seeing a change in a player's habits or a sudden dip in his enthusiasm allowed me to go further with him: Is it family problems? Is he struggling financially? Is he tired? What kind of mood is he in? Sometimes I could even tell that a player was injured when he thought he was fine.

"I don't think many people fully understand the value of observing. I came to see observation as a critical part of my management skills. The ability to see things is key—or, more specifically, the ability to see things you don't expect to see."

Once you assume the role of observing, you will find that there are several strengths being underutilized, several business assumptions that are stunting growth and several blind spots that are unnoticed. These could be at the organizational level, team level or at the individual level. Once you have observed, your job now is to help people learn, change and grow. That is where organizational, team and individual pit stops come handy.

CELEBRATE THOSE WHO 'REFLECT AND THEN ACT'

Look at those whom you celebrate in your organization. If you are like any other organization, you celebrate people who handle crises well. For example, do you celebrate people who suddenly seem to pull sales out of their pocket or those who managed to somehow achieve production numbers despite all odds?

We do not ask the question if the people who managed the crises so well have actually created the crises in the first place. These are people who acted and then reflected and then made the corrections and somehow produced results. Often these results are accompanied by heavy costs in the long run. However, in the short run the successes position these crises managers as heroes of the organization. If you do not want to fall into that trap, you should celebrate people who reflect and act and hence do not create the adrenaline rush and the nail biting excitement that usually accompanies it.

ACTIVATE LEARNING CAPACITIES

We learn from three sources – the past, the present and the future.

After any project or a task or a milestone or a timeline, it is important that a process check is done to learn what enabled success and what caused the gap in performance. Reflecting on past successes helps the organization and individuals to understand their unique success formula. In strategy this is termed as core competence. Similarly learning from past failures helps us to address stunting habits. These process checks can be formalized through structured pit stops.

During a project or a task there is always a danger of becoming task obsessed and forgetting about the process and/ or people sensitivities. Hence, invoking a spontaneous process check in the middle of action helps in reflection and possible corrections. Learning in the present helps to get more out of what we are doing. Unlike learning from the past which is more like a post-mortem, learning from the present enables mid course corrections and goal achievement. Hence midyear review pit stops and mid project review pit stops are extremely important learning opportunities.

While learning from the past and present help in accelerating performance, learning by experimentation helps in exploring the feasibility and effectiveness of 'out of the box' ideas. To begin with, out of box ideas cannot come from those with the baggage of past successes and deeply ingrained habits. However, the reality is we need to get the same people to experiment. So the question is how we address resistance. This is possible only if we construct pit stops with heterogeneous groups. These could mean including people across level, function, location groups within an organization in pit stops on innovation or business planning or managing change. These pit stops wherever appropriate could also include external stakeholders like customers, suppliers, industry experts and academics.

Factor Pit Stops into Organizational and Job Design

While all organizational structures have integrating forums (to take cross functional decisions) and review forums, they are not well thought through or well executed. A serious flaw in most organizational design exercises is a lack of mindset change training on introduction of the new structure. Somehow it is assumed that if a presentation is made on the overall structure and a new role sheet is given to each individual employee, people will automatically realign. This is a naive attitude. This kind of change will not happen just like that. People need to be trained on how to effectively use organizational, team and individual pit stops.

LAP 8 – SECTOR II

HOW SMART IS YOUR ANNUAL APPRAISAL PIT STOP LIKELY TO BE?

How smart is your Annual Appraisal Pit Stop likely to be?

Bhavishyavani for Team Leaders

In the next few pages there are twenty tarot cards. Pick up a number between 1 to 20 at random. Read the tarot card with that number. Each tarot card mentions certain personal characteristics. If the characteristics mentioned in the card that you picked up matches your own characteristics please tick on the card. Then go to the yearly forecast section that follows and refer to the corresponding card to know how smart your annual appraisal pit stop is likely to be. If the characteristics on the tarot card do not adequately describe you, please pick up any other card again at random and go through the process mentioned above.

Tarot Card 1

You like to take responsibility. You think through what has to be done. You consult people but primarily it's your final call. You provide clear directions by telling subordinates what to do and how to do it. You are a hands-on leader and you manage execution tightly. You are someone who gives improvement focused and personalized feedback very often. You are after people to get work done. You rely on discipline and punishment to get the best out of your subordinates.

You consistently achieve high performance. Each of your team members also achieves high performance because you would not accept anything less.

Tarot Card 2

Exceeding expectations is very important to you. You drive yourself and your team very hard. Customers love you as you continuously delight them. You are passionate about your work and hate to let down yourself, your boss or your department.

You spend a lot of time with key internal and external customers and stakeholders. You listen to them, understand their needs and find ways to create superior value for them.

Tarot Card 3

You are considered a good natured person. Your team likes you as you are always helpful in times of trouble and distress. In return people walk the extra mile for you. By being accommodative you motivate people rather than ordering them around. This ensures a committed team that delivers results.

Tarot Card 4

You believe in spotting mistakes and giving critical improvement feedback so that your team members perform well. You do not mince words. Team members are on their toes. They do not take you or their performance lightly.

Tarot Card 5

You like harmony. You care for people's feelings and hence are careful not to hurt them.

Tarot Card 6

You discuss overall performance expectations and goals with each of your team members and let them take responsibility to deliver them. Your leadership philosophy is hands off as you believe people need space to perform. It also gives you the bandwidth to handle discrete responsibilities pertaining to your own role and develop skills to grow into a higher role.

Tarot Card 7

You are task oriented. Your interactions are functional and are focused on getting the task done. When you meet you team members you ask them for an update on specific activities; similarly when your team meets you they know that the conversation is on activities they were supposed to complete. You strongly believe that regular focus on details helps in execution.

Tarot Card 8

You are a logical person who gets into root causes of problems and opportunities. You ask a lot of questions, demand data based discussions and give honest on the face feedback.

Tarot Card 9

You are a energetic leader who builds trusting relations in your team. You have highly engaged team members. People from other units want to work in your team.

Tarot Card 10

Your philosophy is "customer is the king." You practice this philosophy to the tee. You do everything to meet their requirements. Customers know that they can make requests and you will not say no. Often you do more than what you have committed. Obviously your internal and external customers adore you.

Tarot Card 11

Just like any team, in your team you have stars, steady performers and learners. You distribute work based on capabilities and get the best out of each individual.

Tarot Card 12

You are a good follower and align naturally with any boss you work with. You understand their priorities, their style and read their mind regularly to ensure that your work is in line with their thinking and expectations. You regularly consult your boss on important matters and implement those that have his/her blessings.

Tarot Card 13

You have a clear view of how each individual in your team is doing. You classify your team members as high, medium and low performers based on your observations. This classification helps you to map people to various tasks, projects and situations.

Tarot Card 14

Getting high performance is very important for you. You define department priorities, goals and exhort team members to do whatever it takes to achieve goals. In team meetings people who achieve and over achieve their goals are celebrated as Heroes and you come down strongly on those who do not perform. You clearly communicate that less than top performance will not be tolerated and force people to push their performance limits.

Tarot Card 15

You are aware that in a larger organizational context, your team can control and influence only that much. Other teams and departments also have an important role and influence your team's performance.

Hence you share the joys and sorrows of your team members and empathize with their feelings of helplessness when things are not happening as per the plan.

Tarot Card 16

Feelings are complex, difficult to understand and handle. But you know how to manage all this. You know that the essence is to achieve results and at the same time retain team members and keep them happy. Unfortunately this is not easy as it sounds. Your bosses have multiple agendas, HR has its own and each team member their own. Maneuvering through the maze of these contrasting expectations requires positive political management skills and you excel in the same. As you do it for the purpose of the company, it is worth the effort it entails.

Tarot Card 17

You are the warrior leader. In your team there is always action and this is for a noble cause. You and your team are putting down one problem after another. After all isn't management all about removing problems. You are the acknowledged fire-fighting expert of the unit for all critical problems.

Tarot Card 18

You give feedback to your team members throughout the year on their goals and other critical tasks. You help each team member to reflect and learn from each experience. You give honest praise and also dig deeper into what enabled the person to succeed. Similarly you give critical feedback as you care for your team members. Every critical feedback is followed by a thorough root cause analysis.

Tarot Card 19

You believe in helping people to help themselves. You see your role as a catalyst in the process. You help team members to self reflect and self manage their goals. You use facilitative questioning to make them think, do a deeper analysis and gain insights about their talent as well as blocks. You help them to use these insights to enhance their performance. You have a high trusting relationship with each of your team members.

Tarot Card 20

For you, great relationships lead to great team performance. You invest significant amount of time in building deep connections with your team members. Your team swears by you and demonstrates loyalties to you. People support each other and contribute towards the team's high performance.

Your Annual Appraisal Forecast for you

Go to the Tarot Card number that you picked up and read your forecast for this year's annual appraisal.

If **Tarot Card 1** resonates with you, the flip side of your characteristics and your annual appraisal forecast are as follows:

The flip side of your characteristics:

The team may leave all the thinking work to you. Your style may not allow people to make mistakes and hence their learning is limited to following the process you have laid out. Some members may not give their best simply because they know you like to think for them.

Annual Appraisal Prediction for you: You may experience moderate difficulty level during the annual appraisals. Several team members want high ratings, but you know they have not achieved or exceeded expectations on several goals on their own merit. However you cannot raise this as an issue as you poked your nose and did not give them a chance to stand on their feet. On the strength of their performance, they may also be expecting growth. However many of them may not be ready for next levels as they have not learnt to take decisions on their own.

If **Tarot Card 2** resonates with you, the flip side of your characteristics and your annual appraisal forecast are as follows:

The flip side of your characteristics:

Customer focus can compromise your employee focus. You may land up not spending sufficient time engaging with your team members. This may mean that you have more trusting relationships with your customers than your team members.

Annual Appraisal Prediction for you: You may struggle to put together feedback for annual appraisal that is meaningful as you have not given it a thought during the year. When you give feedback as part of performance appraisal, some team members may share openly that you should have given this feedback during the year so that they could have worked on the same. Many may chose to be quiet but they may have similar feelings.

If **Tarot Card 3** resonates with you, the flip side of your characteristics and your annual appraisal forecast are as follows:

The flip side of your characteristics:

At times task urgency may require that you take tough stances. However, your accommodative behavior may come in the way of getting work done.

Annual Appraisal Prediction for you: The development part of your appraisal discussion with your team members will go very well. However the rating part of your appraisal discussion will be challenging with aggressive and assertive team members. Appraisal discussion is about individual's discrete contribution. As you have not been demanding, you may find it difficult to give tough feedback at the end of the year. Some team members may bully you to give higher ratings. You will find it difficult to justify the same with your reporting manager. The ratings may get revised and that may create some unpleasantness with some team members

If **Tarot Card 4** resonates with you, the flip side of your characteristics and your annual appraisal forecast are as follows:

The flip side of your characteristics:

If you are excessively critical, your team members may not demonstrate enough confidence especially in taking key decisions. They also may be uncomfortable in escalating issues that they are not able to handle because of the fear of being reprimanded.

Annual Appraisal Prediction for you: You will have an easy appraisal. When people are under confident it does not take too much effort to make them accept feedback and ratings. However there could be unspoken unhappiness in team members that could impact their engagement levels as well as longevity in the organization. An important challenge that you will face in your own appraisal is lack of clear successors to you from within your team. This may affect your own growth prospects.

If **Tarot Card 5** resonates with you, the flip side of your characteristics and your annual appraisal forecast are as follows:

The flip side of your characteristics:

You may not be bringing out the critical performance issues you have with team members. Hence they may lose out on opportunities for honest feedback and accelerated personal development.

Annual Appraisal Prediction for you: With team members who are conscientious and critically appraise themselves, you will be able to conduct a great appraisal. However team members who have performance blind spots, hidden agendas or an "I am ok-Others need to change" kind of attitude – you will probably have difficult appraisal discussions. You may agree to their ratings as you do not like dissonance. However you will have difficulty justifying such ratings with your reporting manager. You may wonder if it is worth-while to be polite at the cost of your credibility.

If **Tarot Card 6** resonates with you, the flip side of your characteristics and your annual appraisal forecast are as follows:

The flip side of your characteristics:

If you have not set regular review mechanisms in place, you may be in for a rude shock on several goals. Different members would be at different stages of maturity and hence some may require a more hands on leadership support from you at least for some time. You will benefit from a "Horses for Courses" style, that is, a customized style for each team member.

Annual Appraisal Predication for you: You will have a great appraisal with those team members who are good at self management. They would have handled your hands off approach with high responsibility. However those who need external structure may come with excuses on what prevented them from achieving the goals. If you give them lower ratings, which probably you will if you are honest, you will have some heart burns to address.

If **Tarot Card 7** resonates with you, the flip side of your characteristics and your annual appraisal forecast are as follows:

The flip side of your characteristics:

People may not have the 'big picture understanding' of what they are doing and how what are doing is contributing to the business or the goals of the company. Hence they may not be inspired. When there are hurdles around activities, they could very easily get de-motivated as there is no larger vision that serves as an anchor for them during such times.

Annual Appraisal Prediction for you: Your appraisal discussions will go off well with high performers, but you will find it hard to handle conversations with team members whose performance you rate as average. This is because your transactional style of leadership may not have let you find the time for building trusting relationships with your team members. Hence they see their work as another job and will leave you for better prospects. Retaining such employees would be a challenge. Only a compelling vision and an inspiring leader can hold people back.

If **Tarot Card 8** resonates with you, the flip side of your characteristics and your annual appraisal forecast are as follows:

The flip side of your characteristics:

Due to your preoccupation with logic, you may not be sensitive to the feelings of people.

At times people may operate from intuition and may not be able to justify their opinions and decisions. Recent research has indicated that intuition is complex logic. The brain engages in deeper analysis and communicates decisions to the conscious mind. Hence intuitive decisions are of significant value.

Annual Appraisal Prediction for you: You appraisal will be highly value adding as people understand very clearly what they did well and what they could do better. However, during the appraisal, if you do not sense the feelings of people (example: worries about their future) you may not perceive concerns and anxieties or even the excitement and enthusiasm of the appraise, which in turn may come in the way of building trusting relationships.

If **Tarot Card 9** resonates with you, the flip side of your characteristics and your annual appraisal forecast are as follows:

The flip side of your characteristics:

Your team is like an island and your team's culture more of an exception in your unit/ company. Unless you influence your peers and your unit to embrace the highly engaged culture that you have managed to create – the good things that you are doing will die down with you. Also the extent to which the high engagement levels will convert to significantly high performance will remain a question mark as other teams do not practice this style of leadership.

Annual Appraisal Prediction for you: You will have a great annual appraisal discussion with your team members. You have developed deep trusting relations with your team and also have engaged with their performance throughout the year. Be mindful of the bell curve philosophy and position it well within your team. Encourage them to look at it as a way to bench mark themselves with the best in the team and in the company and continuously step up their performance and fully realize their potential. If you distance yourself from relative ratings and take a victim stance, you may actually lose your credibility within the team.

If **Tarot Card 10** resonates with you, the flip side of your characteristics and your annual appraisal forecast are as follows:

The flip side of your characteristics:

You and your team are always under pressure due to tight delivery commitments to your internal and external customers. Such commitments once in a while are fine, but as you make them throughout the year, work life imbalance and fatigue may set in. Team members complain that you should consult them before making commitments and sometimes be assertive in negotiating new timelines with clients and more resource support within the organization.

Annual Appraisal Prediction for you: If your team has created high impact with your internal and external customers, you will have great appraisal discussions. To sustain your fanatical customer orientation you will need to hold a deeper appraisal conversation with each member on how to innovate, how to work on their strengths, address blind spots etc. Otherwise your team will continue to over stretch and break down at some point. As you over commit, your team has a tendency to underperform. Hence while they would have done good work, you will find yourself rating them low. Even where ever you rated them high, you will find it hard to justify the ratings as after all final ratings are data based and not intention based.

If **Tarot Card 11** resonates with you, the flip side of your characteristics and your annual appraisal forecast are as follows:

The flip side of your characteristics:

You may be seen as someone who favors a few over others. While you give critical tasks to your star employees who are most reliable, others may feel that they do not get enough opportunities, encouragement or support to prove that they are on par with the stars.

Annual Appraisal Prediction for you: You have made your choices fairly clear through the kind of projects you gave people through the year. Hence your team members may not experience surprises. Your challenge would be to ensure growth for star performers and to retain steady performers as they feel labeled by you. Under performers may feel that they have never really been given a chance to prove their capabilities.

If **Tarot Card 12** resonates with you, the flip side of your characteristics and your annual appraisal forecast are as follows:

The flip side of your characteristics:

Your team may perceive you only as a postman who delivers messages about decisions rather than a leader capable of taking own decisions. Some of them may even think that you are political, though that may not be your intention. Some team members may also try to cultivate relations with your boss as they know who the real boss is.

Annual Appraisal Prediction for you: You would probably consult your boss on performance and ratings of your team members even before you get into the annual performance discussion. Hence you can be assured of your peace of mind!

While other team leaders may be worried about how to sell ratings of their team members to their reporting managers, you are getting into the discussion with a mandate in place. However as your focus would be on selling pre-decided ratings you may not listen deeply to your team member and/or use any new insights from the appraisee conversation. This may affect the trust levels between you and your team members. You may also lose some members in the process.

If **Tarot Card 13** resonates with you, the flip side of your characteristics and your annual appraisal forecast are as follows:

The flip side of your characteristics:

Your tendency to label people may be causing you to conflate performance with people. Hence you may create a permanent label for each individual in your team which creates blinkers.

Annual Appraisal Prediction for you: As you have already made up your mind about the capabilities of your team member, appraisal discussions are just a formality. Wherever your judgment is in line with reality and is acceptable to the appraisee, you will have a great appraisal discussion. Otherwise the discussion could be a disaster. The appraisee may provide counter evidence to refute your feedback. The overall feeling will be a sense of unfairness.

If **Tarot Card 14** resonates with you, the flip side of your characteristics and your annual appraisal forecast are as follows:

The flip side of your characteristics:

As there is huge performance pressure, team members may stray on company values to meet and exceed goals. A culture of "Just Do it" over rides "It is important how you do it".

Annual Appraisal Prediction for you: You would have an unambiguous discussion on ratings. However the objective of annual appraisal discussion is to understand what enabled success. Enablers include values and behaviours. You will find this discussion difficult to handle as you have never championed means as important as the end result.

It is very likely that the ratings on values will be less than honest. You would be doing disservice to the organization when such people are promoted and they in turn create "What ever it takes" culture. Keep in mind the high profile companies that folded up in recent times. They were proven high performers; it's just that they did not care for values.

If **Tarot Card 15** resonates with you, the flip side of your characteristics and your annual appraisal forecast are as follows:

The flip side of your characteristics:

Team members may refuse to be held accountable for outcomes and want to be measured only on activities that are within their control. Further you may not be able to command respect as they see you as one among the victims of the corporate game.

Annual Appraisal Prediction for you: Please expect a tough time during your appraisal meetings. Team members want to be rated high as they want you to evaluate activity based metrics and not result based metrics. They may also believe that you cannot influence your managers regarding their ratings.

If **Tarot Card 16** resonates with you, the flip side of your characteristics and your annual appraisal forecast are as follows:

The flip side of your characteristics:

People may find you political and read between the lines even if you did not mean anything. In this process, trust is a big casualty.

Annual Appraisal Prediction for you: Your appraisal discussion will be like a game of chess. Both you and your appraisee will make your moves very thoughtfully. Both of you will behave like advocates arguing your respective side of the story. Authenticity, learning and meaningful discussion are out of question

If **Tarot Card 17** resonates with you, the flip side of your characteristics and your annual appraisal forecast are as follows:

The flip side of your characteristics:

Instead of removing fires and celebrating the heroism of each other, for a moment if you stop and look into the root causes, you may find that you and your team are responsible for the fires in the first place. Your linear thinking could be causing the problems. Embracing a holistic understanding and approach could remove the fires altogether.

Constant firefighting creates two tendencies – the first is fatigue and work life imbalance; the second is an addiction to firefighting – if things are going smooth, you and your team starts feeling restless.

Annual Appraisal Prediction for you: You would realize that most of the goals of team members have not been met as everyone has been focused on fire fighting and did not have the time for important things. Even where goals have been met, the quality of achievement may be far from satisfactory. And how can they be? You simply did not have time for reviewing goals during the year.

If **Tarot Card 18** resonates with you, the flip side of your characteristics and your annual appraisal forecast are as follows:

The flip side of your characteristics:

If you over do feedback, team members may feel constantly under scrutiny.

Annual Appraisal Prediction for you: You will have a great annual appraisal dialogue with each member. There are no surprises and to be honest you may not require a formal appraisal discussion as you had several formal and informal ones during the year.

If **Tarot Card 19** resonates with you, the flip side of your characteristics and your annual appraisal forecast are as follows:

The flip side of your characteristics:

At times when you need to talk tough especially with under-performers, you may find it difficult to initiate the conversation.

Annual Appraisal Prediction for you: You will have a WOW appraisal discussion with each of your team members. The development dialogues will be a role model for all. Just be mindful that while absolute ratings are in your control, relative ratings are not. Hence preparing your team member for normalization is very important to sustain the trusting relation you have with them.

If **Tarot Card 20** resonates with you, the flip side of your characteristics and your annual appraisal forecast are as follows:

The flip side of your characteristics:

In a team where people have great relationships, team members tend to tolerate dysfunctional behaviours of various team members, sometimes even compromising team performance. Loyalty to you as the leader may be at the cost of loyalty to the organization.

Annual Appraisal Prediction for you: Your appraisal discussion with your team members will go extremely well as you have invested in building trusting relations with them during the year. Appraisals are occasions where you need to wear two hats – one is that of the team member (which you handle admirably well) and the second is that of management (where you own up and communicate the normalized rating). The management's decision may always not be yours. Your strength of character shines through when you are able communicate the management's decision with conviction, even when you have not bought into it yourself and at the same time are able to reach out to the team members to keep their engagement intact.

ADVICE FROM BHAVISHYAVANI (SOOTHSAYER)

We are after all complex human beings. Several characteristics from several tarots would have resonated with you. Each strength when taken to a high level of excellence also creates a corresponding flip side. For example, if you become an excellent logical thinker, you could miss out on intuitive sensing. You may ask for data everywhere and miss out on gut feeling. Our strength as well as our flip side manifests in the appraisal

meeting and impacts it's outcomes. We need to be aware of the
flip side and not let it convert our strength into a weakness.

How smart is your Annual Appraisal Pit Stop likely to be?

Bhavishyavani for Team Members

Dear Appraisee, do you want to know how your annual appraisal
pit stop forecast? It's simple. Please find below four quadrants.
Each quadrant has attributes that represent a particular way of
thinking and working. Tick all the attributes that you associate
yourself with. If you are curious about how others perceive you,
you may like to seek feedback from your friends and colleagues.

Quadrant 1	Passion, Vision, Logical, Arrogant, Strong Values, Assertive, Energy, Challenging, Aggressive, Positive restlessness, Not willing to shift positions
Quadrant 2	Accepting, Ensure pleasantness, Fear, Subordinate, Empathy, Listening, Caring, Accommodate, Celebrating others, Giving in, Maybe I have the wrong attitude, Deference to authority
Quadrant 3	Compromise, Adherence to status quo, Not giving space for dialogue, Neither taking the lead nor letting others take the lead
Quadrant 4	Long term focus, Trust, Patronize, Collaborate, Address what is in it for each other, No hidden agendas, Collaborate

You will have by now identified which quadrant represents
more of you. Now are you anxious to know your bhavisyavani
as an appraisee? No more wait time. Here it is. Go straight to the
corresponding quadrant on the next page.

Quadrant 1: I Win	Quadrant 2: You Win
You revel in making others agree to your point of view. You approach logically and are assertive in putting your viewpoints across. For you winning is so important that you may be touchy about tough feedback. You may also look at feedback from the prism of how it would impact your ratings. If your appraiser is like you he/she will approach the appraisal interview in a combative mode. Expect a full-fledged war. If your appraiser is non-assertive, he/she will be scared to give you honest feedback. May agree to your self-ratings and adjust them in normalization.	You readily agree. Maybe you see others point of view faster than others. Maybe you are highly reflective. But one may wonder how come you never advocate your point of view and how come you own interests never matter to you. If your appraiser is opposite to you, already you may have given up on your appraisal conversation. If your appraiser is understanding in nature he/she may focus on what you did right and help you to be fair with yourself.

Quadrant 3: No One Wins	Quadrant 4: We Win
You do not care for winning. You also do not care for others winning. Compromise is your preferred option. If your appraiser is combative you probably will resist actively or passively either in the appraisal discussion or afterwards. If your appraiser is non-assertive, he/she will actively resist during the discussion. As you do not believe in any change, your appraiser may actually be thinking of how to make you part of of his/her past.	You know that your truth is partial and are willing to put your viewpoint forward and listen to others. For you building trusting relations and getting the best from yourself and others is very important. You do not take the entire credit and always acknowledge others contributions. If your appraiser is like you, you will have a healthy conversation. Due to your intent, you can change the tone of a combative appraiser from outright aggression to an appreciative dialogue. You never take advantage of a non-assertive appraiser as it neither helps you nor him/her in the long run.

Lap 8 – Sector III

Test Drive your Trust Performance Quotient

Congratulations on your decision to become a Leader of Choice and manage your pit stops effectively. Do you want to find for yourself the extent to which you are a Leader of Choice right now?

If yes, please go ahead and answer this self-reflection instrument. Read one statement at a time and tick against the rating scale that is most applicable to you. If you can recollect instances that justify the rating, you are on the right track. As you are using this instrument for reflection and development, be harsh on yourself. Against each statement write either 'Always' or 'Sometimes' or 'Rarely' based on what is representative of who you are.

Cultivate the Smell of the Place (Attitudes)

PILLAR 1: RESPECT

I listen with an open mind even when a person is putting forward a completely contrary view to mine.

Evidence

I find opportunities with my team members to demonstrate that I care.

Evidence

I celebrate each team member's unique talent.

Evidence

I openly acknowledge if a team member has an idea which is better than what I had in mind.

Evidence

I keep my negative emotions in check in difficult situations.

Evidence

PILLAR 2: FAIRNESS

I customize my leadership based on individual member aspirations, talents and needs.

Evidence

I help each member to discover and utilize their strengths.

Evidence

I stand by my team members if I see any injustice happening.

Evidence

I do not speak (ill of) behind any one's back.

Evidence

I differentiate based on performance and not based on personality.

Evidence

PILLAR 3 - AUTHENTICITY

I share my personal stories as leadership experiences for people to learn.

Evidence

I live by my values even when in certain situations it puts me to a disadvantage.

Evidence

I self reflect, admit mistakes and make changes in my personal attitudes and behaviors.

Evidence

I share my true feelings with team members.

Evidence

I regularly invest time in deep personal bonding with my team.

Evidence

Build High Performance Engine (Skills)

PILLAR 4: PLAN AND EXECUTE

I plan the goals of my department and team members in a thoughtful manner.

Evidence

I ensure detailed micro planning of each goal and the nature of support required.

Evidence

I ensure focus of the team on customer and outcomes.

Evidence

I share my performance expectations with each team member and am ruthless about delivery.

Evidence

I plan for contingencies and am well prepared if they were to occur.

Evidence

PILLAR 5: REVIEW AND LEARN

I hold regular formal and informal reviews with my team members on progress of their goals.

Evidence

I focus on "how" the member is accomplishing the goal as much as "what" the person has accomplished.

Evidence

I ensure that review meetings are learning opportunities and not assessment events.

Evidence

I encourage members to learn from mistakes.

Evidence

During the review sessions I critique if the goal is relevant or there is a need to replace the goal.

Evidence

PILLAR 6: GROWTH

I discuss aspirations, talents with team members and consciously scout for opportunities to realize them.

Evidence

I challenge team member's paradigms that may come in the way of their growth.

Evidence

I promote my team member's talent with my peers and senior managers.

Evidence

I create opportunities for team members to learn new skills and coach them where ever appropriate.

Evidence

I invest time in preparing detailed career plans for my team members and regularly review progress.

Evidence

Reflect on all the six pillars of Trust-Performance. All pillars need to be strong to build a stable house. Similarly all the six pillars of Trust-Performance are critical to become a "Leader of Choice" and leverage pit stop opportunities to the fullest.

MY STRONGEST PILLAR

Ideas to further build and sustain this pillar (here identify a statement related to your strength pillars where you need improvement):

_____

_____

_____

_____

MY WEAKEST PILLAR

Ideas to build and strengthen this pillar: (here identify a statement related to your weak pillars on which you want to focus as priority).

_____

_____

_____

_____

LAP 9

PIT STOP MAGIC

Lap 9 – Sector I
Trust, Pit Stops and Performance

Do you remember the magical run of Usain Bolt in the Beijing Olympics? While he ran faster in the Berlin World Athletics meet, I want to take you through this for the sheer magic. He did not have a great start, was trailing midway, takes off at 40 meters and between 80 meters and the finish line was able to look at the clock, put both his hands to his sides, thump his chest and clock 9.69 seconds, way ahead of Richard Thomson who clocked a distant 9.89 seconds. Wasn't that incredible? There was no effort.

Take a closer look at the person. He is 6.5, not short, strong and stocky to be a great sprinter. Bolt's running suffers from technical faults, most glaringly at the start. In the Beijing final only Churandy Martina reacted to the starter's pistol slower than the man who was about to set the world record. He has been labeled as lazy, sleeps on the day of the race, eats whatever he can get his hands on, has nuggets before the race. How can this person be a world-beater?

In an interview immediately after beating a world record he was asked what contributes to his winning. He said something wonderful. He said he feels good about himself and that makes him win.

That's the secret. With all the apparent weaknesses, Bolt still wins because he feels good about himself.

When people feel good about themselves they give in their best. They are not concerned about whether they will perform or not. They do not worry about their weaknesses. They stay glued to their strengths and convert that into top talent.

Get on to YouTube and see the video of Bolt at the beginning of the race. You find him having a lot of fun. It's almost as if he knows that he is going to win. He seems to consider the race an arena for dancing with joy and not as a life and death situation. Because he wants to have fun, he does not seem to be burdened by past success or failure.

To become a Leader of Choice we need to stop asking the question "How to make my team members work?" and start asking "How to create a work environment that makes it easy for people to use their talent?" When we change the question we ask we are changing the lenses from which we as leaders look at our team members. Once we assume talent, we focus on creating the right cultural environment that makes people feel good about their talent. When people feel good about themselves, performance will happen automatically.

Talent by definition is what comes out effortlessly. This means the knowledge, skills and attitudes applied effortlessly. Hence it is called unconscious competence. If you ask highly talented people what enabled their success, they generally talk about good luck. You may assume that they are being modest. However, the reality is that they themselves may not know how their strengths and weaknesses combine in ways in which talent emerges that is unique to them. That is why if you were a Manager of Usain Bolt, you may be tempted to work on his laziness, which is an obvious weakness and probably is stunting his full potential. In looking at his weakness in isolation, you may inadvertently be killing his talent. His laziness is an essential ingredient to his talent and in his success. To become a Leader of Choice you need to understand the DNA of a person's talent, not a list of the person's strengths and weaknesses. When you do this, the team member starts feeling valued. This is the first pillar for trust building.

When people are successful by demonstrating their talent, one factor, which influences their success, is the environment. There are rules that people learn and master about the environment. These rules become axioms. As the environment – both internal and external, changes a person has to become aware of the new rules. When he does not or chooses not to, the unconscious competence that contributed to the person's success now converts into unconscious incompetence. Effortless talent now becomes effortless non-talent. The leader's role is to help the team member to become aware and embrace the new rules. This is possible only if the team member believes that the leader has his (the team member's) interest in mind. Only then the team member will perceive the leader to be fair. The role of pit stops – whether at the organizational, team or individual levels is to celebrate a person's unconscious competence and bring in awareness when external or internal environment rules change.

As we learnt, this is the second pillar of trust building.

Does it make a difference in terms of what you contribute and how you contribute, when you treat your office as a home? If yes, will it also make a difference if you treat your team member not just as a professional but also as a person? When you treat your team member as a person, you start valuing her aspirations, her home context and cultural diversity. This results in honest conversations and builds authentic relations – the third pillar of trust building. Now you have a team member who wants to work for you, give in her best and prove worthy of being part of your team. Do you need to put in effort to get high performance? Not really.

My Friend, when you start working on all these fronts I have discussed in the book, you have started your journey towards becoming the Leader of Choice.

And lo and behold, your pit stops have transformed into high leverage opportunities to win the most important race of your life.

An Invitation to Partner

Dear Reader,

I hope that your pit stop to read this book was useful. I started with an idea and built this along the way. I would be fooling myself if I think that this book is perfect or complete. It is neither.

I am soon planning to release the second edition of this book. I invite your valued addition in the form of stories, personal examples, best practices and new chapters. I will acknowledge all contributions in the next edition. We will send gift vouchers as honorarium to those whose value additions form part of the second edition.

Look forward to your feedback as well as value addition. Please write to me at kanti@institutionbuilders.com.

A Big Thank You

Friends whom I associated with in the pit stop thinking process:

Mahrukh Bandorawalla   It is always a pleasure to work with Mahrukh. She is a bright OD consultant and knows how to get the best out of a maverick like me.

Amitabh Babbar   He is the best performance management consultant that I know of and stands tall in front of HR charlatans with big titles. He has a knack of creating value out of any idea.

Anuradha Rajan   Anuradha has painstakingly edited this book. I only had an idea. She brought the idea to life. Her writing and editing skills ensured that each chapter and paragraph explained the idea eloquently.

Ambar Sheikh   Ambar is a spirited individual with a big heart and bigger dreams. She supported Marukh and me on the 'Pit Stops for Peak Performance project'. Without her association, the Institution Builders vehicle would not have taken off.

Kopal Garg   An intelligent intern who helped us in testing the idea of cartoons to communicate ideas. She now works for Cap Gemini. Kopal is a tough lady who made a difference to Institution Builders and the pit stop book.

Nida Shahid   Nida helped in creating the appraisal cartoon story. She is an expert in Organization Assessment and Leader Development. We worked on several OD projects together. She is a combination of great thinking and execution skills.

Jaya Jaiswani   Jaya made the Pit Stop book look smart. She represents the next generation HR talent. With a high emotional quotient, she handles OD projects of Institution Builders.

Aditya Gopal and Shrestha Gopal Aditya and Shreshtha designed the initial front cover page. They both are creative and believe in the value of excellence.

Karisma Nanavati A budding filmmaker and a fashion designer, she knows how to make people look good. My photo on the author's page is courtesy Karisma.

Great Place to Work Institute India Their vision of 'India as a Great Place to Work and Live' inspires me to give in my best in my consulting work. Several of the best practices quoted in this book are those I learnt as part of my association with them.

Gyanodaya and Performance Management Group of Aditya Birla Company My creative juices of Pit Stops for Peak Performance are a result of consulting work and collaboration with friends and well wishers such as Pratik Roy, Anupama Mohan, Niladri Roy, Amitabh Babbar, Saurabh Choudhari, Nagma Malim, Sujatha Sudheendra, Anupama Basu, Internal Trainers of Aditya Birla Group and ABG's External Trainers who championed the pit stop movement.

And a big 'thank you' to Sounak Chakrabarty who gave Institution Builders its purpose He is one of the best minds I have experienced and is a promising OD talent of the country. His presence in the formative years of our organization helped us to do quality work and win enduring client relationships. His coaching pit stops helped me to stay focussed on our purpose till date.

SIGNING OFF THE FIRST EDITION WITH
NIDA SHAHID's SKETCH OF A PIT STOP

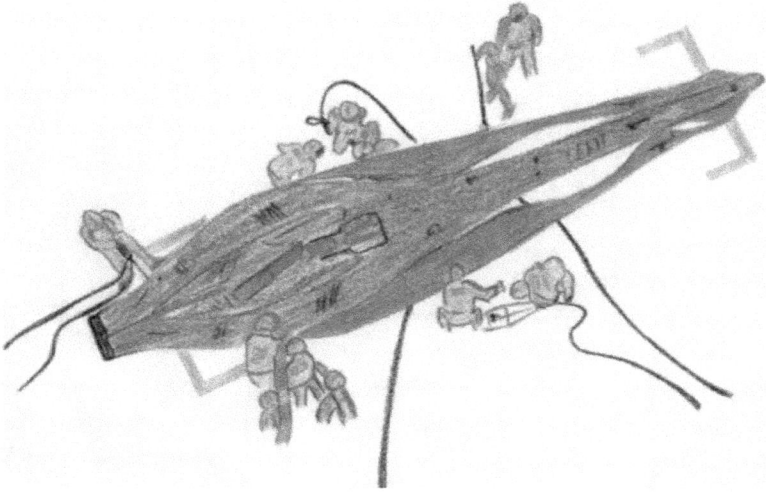

About Institution Builders

We are a new age strategic HR consulting firm. We specialize in change solutions using whole systems thinking and methodologies. Whether it is design and implementation of performance management system or leadership development or vision deployment or cultural change or merger integration or implementation of total quality or wasteful cost elimination, we use whole systems approaches to engage the entire organization in real time and bring rapid change.

While conventional change management approaches fail to engage everyone in an organization simultaneously, whole systems approaches not only evoke the active participation of all employees but deliver measurable and sustainable outcomes within a short time.

Institution Builders
Enabling democracy in business